ALAN AYCKBOURN
IN CHEKHOV'S FOOTSTEPS

A Study of Chekhovian Character Traits in Ayckbourn Drama

Mustafa Kirca

ALAN AYCKBOURN IN CHEKHOV'S FOOTSTEPS

A Study of Chekhovian Character Traits in Ayckbourn Drama

ibidem-Verlag
Stuttgart

Bibliografische Information der Deutschen Nationalbibliothek
Die Deutsche Nationalbibliothek verzeichnet diese Publikation in der Deutschen Nationalbibliografie; detaillierte bibliografische Daten sind im Internet über http://dnb.d-nb.de abrufbar.

Bibliographic information published by the Deutsche Nationalbibliothek
Die Deutsche Nationalbibliothek lists this publication in the Deutsche Nationalbibliografie; detailed bibliographic data are available in the Internet at http://dnb.d-nb.de.

Coverbild: ©Klicker / PIXELIO

Gedruckt auf alterungsbeständigem, säurefreien Papier
Printed on acid-free paper

ISBN-10: 3-8382-0018-7
ISBN-13: 978-3-8382-0018-7

© *ibidem*-Verlag
Stuttgart 2010

Alle Rechte vorbehalten

Das Werk einschließlich aller seiner Teile ist urheberrechtlich geschützt. Jede Verwertung außerhalb der engen Grenzen des Urheberrechtsgesetzes ist ohne Zustimmung des Verlages unzulässig und strafbar. Dies gilt insbesondere für Vervielfältigungen, Übersetzungen, Mikroverfilmungen und elektronische Speicherformen sowie die Einspeicherung und Verarbeitung in elektronischen Systemen.

All rights reserved. No part of this publication may be reproduced, stored in or introduced into a retrieval system, or transmitted, in any form, or by any means (electronic, mechanical, photocopying, recording or otherwise) without the prior written permission of the publisher. Any person who does any unauthorized act in relation to this publication may be liable to criminal prosecution and civil claims for damages.

Printed in Germany

To Füsun & Arda

CONTENTS

PREFACE (by Dr. Ünal Norman)	1
ACKNOWLEDGEMENTS	3
INTRODUCTION	5
INERTIA	11
Sterile and Parasitic Individuals	16
Pervading Atmosphere	28
FRUSTRATION	31
Frustrating Forces	41
Fantasy Worlds	43
ALIENATION	49
Indifferent Individuals	55
Inadequate Language and Non-Communication	63
Disconnected Dialogue	69
Self-Estrangement	74
VICIOUS CIRCLE	79
Choosing to Be	82
CONCLUSION	85
BIBLIOGRAPHY	89
INDEX	93

PREFACE

Alan Ayckbourn is one of the most prolific and widely performed of the English language playwrights, and a highly esteemed theatre director. He is often described as "King of Giggles". He is critically underestimated due to the influence of the heavily farcical style of his early plays. In America he is still regarded as a boulevard farceur, or simply a clever deviser of intricate stage sets. Although he is knighted for the invaluable work he does for the British theatre, he is still not ranked alongside Harold Pinter, Tom Stoppard or David Hare, who write about important issues of the world. The world of Ayckbourn's plays is smaller and more familiar. The plays depict the domestic foibles of suburban bourgeoisie, exposing their frustrations, disappointments and inadequacies. He has probed into the miserable human lives, the cruelty people unknowingly inflict on each other, and their efforts to come into terms with their failed illusions behind the seemingly happy facades. He does all that with a delicate balance of laughter and pain, and that is his *forte*. Ayckbourn aimed to bring in a fine mix of comedy and tragedy into his plays from the very beginning of his career. He has been committed to exploring serious themes without giving up on the laughter. His *Guru* has been Anton Chekhov. In several interviews he pronounced that he would like to write serious comedies in the Chekhovian vein. Chekhov's defeated, lethargic and pathetic characters skirt around the tragedy of their wasted lives. They are preoccupied with their commonplace, drab and narrow existence with only occasional interval of short lived happiness. We often encounter them in the midst of their feeble struggles, or already defeated, facing an impasse. Mustafa Kırca, in this work, carefully traces and analyses the affinities between the characters of Chekhov and Ayckbourn, and witnesses how one great mind inspires yet another great one. The book will be of interest for teachers, students and theatergoers, and for anyone who wonders, like Shakespeare's Puck, "Lord, what fools these mortals be!"

Dr. Ünal Norman
Middle East Technical University

ACKNOWLEDGEMENTS

This project has been developed out of my studies on Alan Ayckbourn drama submitted as a thesis at Middle East Technical University in Ankara. I am greatly indebted to Assoc. Prof. Dr. Ünal Norman for her invaluable help and guidance throughout the study, and also for her constant moral support and encouragement. I should extend my sincere thanks to Prof. Dr. Meral Çileli and Assoc. Prof. Dr. Necla Çıkıgil for their positive and reassuring attitude and suggestions. An earlier version of the discussion on the use of language in Ayckbourn's plays has previously been published in *Journal of Drama Studies* as "Language in Ayckbourn's Plays" (vol 2, no 2, 2008). I would like to thank Prof. Bhim S. Dahia for his kindly permission to reproduce the material here in this book. I should also thank Dr. Neslihan Yetkiner for her kindly permission to reproduce my article "Dissatisfaction in Ayckbourn Drama" previously published in *Researches on Literature and Stylistics* (Izmir University of Economics, 2009). My thanks are also forwarded to Dr. Nil Korkut, for her sincere encouragements and invaluable comments, and to Dr. Bilal Kırkıcı, for being ready to help whenever I felt the need and for being a patient listener and the reader of the early manuscripts. Finally, I offer my deepest gratitude to Füsun, who has always been a valuable source of comfort and support and has smoothed this path for me.

INTRODUCTION

Modern British dramatist, Alan Ayckbourn is always described as "a man of theater". It is well known that he has worked in theater as a stage manager, actor, writer and director. His own career as an actor and director is thought to have provided experience for him as a playwright (Kalson, 89). With his plays still increasing in number, he is surely one of the most prolific of British playwrights. Alan Ayckbourn has never denied the influences of other writers on his drama; on the contrary, it is safe to say that he has always looked for the ways to make use of other dramatists' influences in composing his own plays. He has not become the imitator of any playwright; yet, he admits that he has been greatly influenced by Pinter's "use of language and his careful selection of words [...] so eloquent, so delicate" and by "Pirandello and Ionesco and Anouilh" (qtd. in Watson, 84); "then of course there's Chekhov and Ibsen, who were huge influences," admits Ayckbourn (qtd. in Dukore, 10).

Particularly, Chekhov's influence on Ayckbourn's drama is born out of a deliberate aim of the dramatist. In an interview, he puts forward that he aspires to write a comedy in Chekhovian manner. He says: "I'd like to finish up writing tremendously human comedies —Chekhovian comedy in a modern way" (qtd. in Page, 135). A few years later, he pronounces: "I want to move further into the Chekhovian field, exploring attitudes to death, loneliness, etc. —themes not generally dealt with in comedy" (qtd. in Page, 135). While creating "human comedies" which he hopes eventually to achieve, it can be argued that Ayckbourn has been inspired by Chekhov's understanding of comedy. Chekhov's plays are usually interpreted on the stage as tragedy, yet Chekhov insistently calls them "comedy, and in places even a farce" (qtd. in Magarshack, 264). The misinterpretation is due to Chekhov's ability to give "the comic twist" to the tragic themes of his plays, combining "dreadful realities" with the ridiculous. Ayckbourn's endeavor to reflect dreadful realities together with laughter in his plays brings him very close to Chekhov and he uses it as effectively.

Ayckbourn pronounces this aim very early in his career, and through the years he has remained committed to this in that his plays of any period, even the most recent ones, carry at least one aspect of Chekhov's impact. Ayckbourn's first published play, *Relatively Speaking* (1967), is based on the general misunderstandings of the characters which give rise to laughter; and with its misunderstanding and farcical elements, this first play labels Ayckbourn as a "traditional farceur," "giving him the reputation of being the most undemanding of entertainers. This initial reputation has obscured the depth and the seriousness of some of his plays" (Page, 134). In this farcical style, nonetheless, Ayckbourn succeeds in treating serious themes as male insensitivity, female inadequacy, and a lack of genuine understanding between the couples within a marriage. Ayckbourn, in his succeeding plays, has developed this style of representing serious themes in light comedies. "Heavy, no; serious, yes," he argues in his preface to *Absent Friends*, objecting to "the mistaken belief that because it's funny, it can't be serious" (*Friends*, 3). He begins to thicken his plots dealing with darker themes —mainly destructive side of marriage, lack of communication, human failure, etc. Critics agree on the idea that the theme may be a very dark one in an Ayckbourn play but it can still evoke laughter from very bitter topics such as homicide, bribery, mental breakdown and the attempt of an unfulfilled housewife to commit suicide, etc. His later comedies prove Ayckbourn's capability of handling tragic themes within a comic framework. The union of comedy with painful events appears in Ayckbourn's more recent plays like *House* and *Garden* as well. Richard Zoglin regards this union as the characteristic of all Ayckbourn plays. He contends: "The laughs are plentiful, but the comedy, as usual in Ayckbourn, is tinged with pathos and pain" (*Time* 60).

The present study argues that the union of laughter with pain in Ayckbourn's drama is conveyed through his characterization contrary to that of farce. In farce, there are flat characters, "all sharp lines with primary colors and cartoon-like". Ayckbourn reversed this style of creating dramatic people in his work; and he gets "closer in his characterisation to [...] serious farceur: Chekhov" (Baker, 34). Chekhov is famous for his realistic character portrayal with psychological depth, a deep understanding of human nature, which enables audiences to identify themselves with these characters. Ayckbourn, too, manages to reflect his characters true to life despite the farcical style of his plays: "it can be funny, but let's make it truthful," he suggests in his preface to *Absent Friends* (*Friends*, 3). He puts great emphasis on realistic rather than stereotypical character portrayal to make his comedies more truthful with credible dramatic people and to make his audiences identify themselves with the characters. With this quality of his plays, "he prompts us to laugh, then to care about the character and to make a connection with ourselves, our own behaviour" (Page, 136). His characters are created with respectable traits of their own, which is in accordance with Chekhov's proposition: "Each character must possess individual features and idiosyncrasies and must speak in a language of his own" (qtd. in Baker, 35). Just as Chekhov's characters are, Ayckbourn's characters, too, are "quickly and indelibly defined; once we get to know them we would not even need the conventional character designations in reading the play to know who is speaking" (Baker, 35). In the present study, I claim that Ayckbourn portrays his characters with the Chekhovian character traits while creating characters contrary to the farcical style of his plays. He dramatizes "real people in real trouble" (Page, 143) —inactive, unfulfilled, and isolated people. In the light of all this, the aim of this book is to show that Ayckbourn is influenced by Chekhov in portraying his dramatis personae as inert, frustrated, and alienated individuals.

This book intends to discuss the impact of Chekhovian character traits on the character portrayal of Ayckbourn's drama. I argue that Chekhov, in his four-act plays, draws his characters with certain outstanding idiosyncrasies; his plays are populated with people who are inactive, lifeless, unfulfilled, disappointed and alienated. He reflects the ordinary human failure in order to show people "how badly you live, how tiresome you are". Ayckbourn's characters are drawn with the same Chekhovian traits. They are equally unhappy individuals, for they are equally lethargic, slow, dissatisfied, tongue-tied and isolated people that allow the playwright to point out how badly man lives, and how tiresome he is. This kind of characterization with certain pathos establishes the perfect equilibrium between farce and tragedy as John L. Styan contends that "farce, which prohibits compassion for human weakness, and tragedy, which demands it, are close kin"; and to support his view Styan refers to *The Cherry Orchard* as "a play which treads the tightrope between them, and results in the ultimate form of that special dramatic balance we know as Chekhovian comedy" (197). This study further argues that Ayckbourn, following Chekhov's footsteps, is good at that tightrope walk between comedy and tragedy, and "if anything, Ayckbourn is more successful than Chekhov in maintaining that balance of the absurd and the substantial" (Baker, 34).

In order to show Chekhov's influence on Ayckbourn's plays at different phases of his drama, plays from different periods of Ayckbourn's writing are chosen. Nonetheless, the selection is carried out with great care so as to cover specifically the plays written after the period when Ayckbourn especially darkened the themes of his plays, *Absent Friends* being the turning point. *Absent Friends* can be said to be different from his earlier plays in that Ayckbourn handles his serious themes in a comic vein masterfully in this play. Serious themes kept appearing in Ayckbourn's theatre during the following years with *Just Between Ourselves* and *Joking*

Apart. Ayckbourn referred to these plays as "winter plays" because of their sad themes blended with a comic framework (Billington, 1990), so these later sad comedies cover a span of the publication of Ayckbourn's winter plays with themes "concerned with total lack of understanding, with growing old and with spiritual and mental collapse," as Ayckbourn explains it in his preface to *Just Between Ourselves*, the first of the winter plays (*Ourselves*, 7). With the "winter plays," Ayckbourn's plays have grown darker and more complex to the point that they could scarcely be called comedies —just as Chekhov's *The Cherry Orchard* or *The Seagull* cannot be called comedies.

Ayckbourn is a prolific dramatist; therefore, as many plays as possible are chosen so as to prove Chekhov's influence on his drama as intentional and pervasive. Furthermore, as Ayckbourn is not a direct imitator of Chekhov, it is not likely to find a Chekhovian impact on every one of his plays. While one play conveys one aspect of Chekhovian influence, another may contain a different aspect. The following plays are selected as having representative Chekhovian character traits: *Absent Friends* (1974), *Just Between Ourselves* (1976), *Joking Apart* (1978), *Season's Greetings* (1980), *Woman in Mind* (1986), *A Small Family Business* (1987), and *Henceforward* (1987) (dates refer to the first performances). The plays will be referred as *Friends*, *Ourselves*, *Apart*, *Greetings*, *Mind*, *Business*, and *Henceforward* respectively throughout the citations in the book. On the other hand, from Chekhov's drama, only his four mature plays, "Big Fours," are included to define the general Chekhovian character traits: *The Seagull* (1898), *Uncle Vanya* (1900), *The Three Sisters* (1901), and *The Cherry Orchard* (1903). The plays will be referred as *Seagull*, *Vanya*, *Sisters* and *Orchard* in the citations.

INERTIA

Chekhov wrote "I despise laziness, as I despise weakness and inertia in mental activity" (qtd. in Eekman, 159). However, all his characters are intentionally portrayed as lazy and inert individuals in that "laziness, mental as well as physical, is a birth defect of many of Chekhov's characters" (Eekman, 147). Chekhov, in his mature plays, portrays his characters as idle individuals who lack the necessary energy to perform any action. Alan Ayckbourn's characters are similarly reflected with certain lack of energy needed for action following the Chekhovian trait, and the playwright creates his dramatis personae with the same Chekhovian character trait of inertia. Both playwrights' characters are immobile in a state of eternal rest. "Nobody is in a hurry," states Maurice Valency, portraying "the usual Chekhovian character [as] a half-hearted participant in an action that barely excites his interest" (189). Ayckbourn's characters, too, in general feel no urgency to do anything; they seem languid and motionless, or if they are in motion, they continue in the same direction, in a straight line and in a leisurely-fashion due to their Chekhovian character trait of inertia.

Although laziness is a birth defect of them, Chekhov's characters endlessly talk about the laziness of mankind and the necessity for work. They always philosophize but do nothing to activate their thoughts. It is a call they believe in at the time they pronounce these words "but they usually forget soon after and they never put it into practice" (Eekman, 145). The importance of working is emphasized in *The Three Sisters* but we know that none of the sisters are eager to carry out what they believe:

> Man must work by the sweat of his brow whatever his class, and that should make up the whole meaning and purpose of his life and happiness and contentment [...] All this longing for work ... Heavens!
>
> (*Sisters*, 252-253)
>
> We must work, work! The reason we fell depressed and take such a gloomy view of life is that we've never known what it is to make a real effort. We're the children of parents who despised work.
>
> (*Sisters*, 268)

There is a strong resistance to motion and change in Chekhov's and Ayckbourn's plays, although their characters are unsatisfied with their mechanical and meaningless lives. They know that their lives are dreary and wasted; yet they are passive dreamers, not doers. Therefore, they are proved to be inactive when they constantly complain of their present situation but do nothing in turn to change it; nor do they make any plans to make it better. *The Cherry Orchard* exemplifies Chekhovian inertia with the landowners, Liubov and Gayev, for instance. The orchard has to be sold to pay its debts. The landowners do not want to lose it, but do nothing to save it. They are evasive when it comes to deciding on the orchard as can be understood from Luibov and Gayev's disconnected responses below:

> Lopakhin: We must decide once and for all: time won't wait. After all, my question's quite simple one. Do you consent to lease your land for villas, or don't you? You can answer in one word: yes or no? Just one word!
> Liubov: Who's been smoking such abominable cigars here?
> Gayev: How very convenient it is having a railway here. (Sits down) Here we are —we have been up to town for lunch and

we're back home already. I pot the red into the middle pocket!
I'd like to go indoors now and have just one game.
Liubov: You've plenty of time.

(*Orchard*, 357)

The landowners lack the motivation to act accordingly and are ruled by their ineptitude even though they return to their estate to save it from the auction. Till the auction of the orchard, they are unable to develop a plan of action; they just wait in vain for an external stimulus that will put them in motion.

Ayckbourn's men and women are similarly regarded as dormant individuals since they lack the power to realize their desires. His female characters, for instance, are unsatisfied with their marriages, yet they are deprived of the vigour to make their marital lives better or to get rid of them altogether. Diana in *Absent Friends*, Vera in *Just Between Ourselves*, and Susan in *Woman in Mind* are the victims of unhappy marriages but none of them can assert the strength of ending off their marriages. Pouring a cream jug over her husband's head is the only point Diana can reach. Vera can only merge into an utter silence at the end, and Susan can only escape to her fantasy husband. They dramatize the same kind of inertia when they show no tendency to action although they desire to launch a carrier, discontent with being housewives. When Susan blurts out in *Woman in Mind* that she lacks "a proper job" (*Mind*, 11), it is her inertia that hampers her, nothing else.

Besides physical inertia of the playwright's women characters, Ayckbourn's male characters are mentally and emotionally inert people without the ability and willingness to understand their wives or meet their needs. They are as paralyzed as those of Chekhov's, particularly when it comes to understanding each other. This creates the "uncomprehending husband" figures in Ayckbourn's drama; his male characters are emotionally insensitive husbands to their wives' feelings and they refuse to understand their female counterparts. This shows the emotional vacuum they live in. In *Absent Friends*, Paul is reminded how romantic he was once toward Diana, but with his insensitive response quoted below, he now proves his unwillingness to be tender to his wife:

> Colin: [...] at the end of the meal, do you know what he did — and this shows how romantic he is underneath all that lot —he picked up that napkin that you'd been using, Di, and he put it in his pocket. Took it home to remind him of you.
> [...]
> Paul: I've just remembered. I've still got that table napkin of hers, you know. [...] I use it to clean my car with.
> (Diana rises, picks up the cream jug and pours it slowly over Paul's head. Paul sits for a moment, stunned).
>
> (*Friends*, 38)

The plays of both dramatists occasionally offer some exceptional characters who convey a sense of energy. These personages in Chekhov's plays "seem to belong to another world than the rest of the cast" (Valency, 189). Particularly, Lopakhin in *The Cherry Orchard* is Chekhov's well-known character with an upward social movement, a former serf turned into a millionaire. Unlike other Chekhov people, he is full of life energy and has power to perform action. Although his forefathers were serfs, he has managed to free himself and become a successful businessman. He is now a practical businessman who can eventually buy the orchard and turn it into lots for cottages:

> If only my father and grandfather could rise from their graves and see everything that's happened ... how their Yermolai, their much-beaten, half-literate Yermolai, the lad that used to run about with bare feet in the winter ... how he's bought this estate, the most beautiful place on God's earth! Yes, I've bought the very estate where my father and grandfather were serfs, where they weren't even admitted to the kitchen!
>
> (*Orchard*, 384)

Nevertheless, "he too is comically inept when it comes to romance" (Senelick, 121). Chekhov would not let even Lopakhin to be an all-round achiever. Varia and Lopakhin are matched together by Liubov for marriage but Lopakhin is impotent to propose marriage to her:

> Liubov: [...] I'd been hoping to get her married to you ... and everything seemed to show that you meant to marry her, too. She loves you, and you must be fond of her, too ... and I just don't know, I just don't know why you seem to keep away from each other. I don't understand it.
> Lopakhin: Neither do I myself, I must confess. It's all so strange somehow. ... If there is still time, I'm ready even now. ... Let's settle it at once —and get it over! Without you here, I don't feel I shall ever propose to her.
>
> (*Orchard*, 394)

The laziness among the characters is infectious, likely spreading to others and quickly influencing them, too. In *Uncle Vanya*, when Yeliena comes to Vanya estate with the Professor, her inertia catches the other characters, too. Sonya accuses her: "Boredom and idleness are infectious. Look: Uncle Vanya isn't doing anything either, just following you about like a shadow, and I've left my work and come running to you to have a chat. I've grown quite lazy, I can't help it" (*Vanya*, 218). Yeliena becomes the embodiment of idleness in Chekhov's drama. Astrov, after Sonya, draws attention to Yeliena's idleness and its being infectious:

> You just happened to come along with your husband and all of us here, who'd been working and running around and trying to create something. We all had to drop everything and occupy ourselves wholly with you and your husband's gout. You two infected all of us with your indolence.
>
> (*Vanya*, 240)

Such an idle life of Chekhov's characters is not commendable of course as it is said that "[a]n idle life can't be virtuous" (*Vanya*, 210). The characters in utter boredom doing nothing purposeful or useful are rusting to become superfluous men and women, and "it is decay caused by inertia" (*Vanya*, 223).

Sterile and Parasitic Individuals

Being powerless to act, Chekhov's and Ayckbourn's characters become sterile individuals who are incapable of producing anything meaningful on their own. The cumulative effect of Chekhov's drama is one of sterility in that all his characters are in the state of being daft and inactive through idleness and disuse of their physical and/or mental faculties. Ayckbourn's portrayal of unproductive characters bears the traces of Chekhovian sterile individuals. He especially reflects his women characters as unproductive people who do not have a proper job of their own due to their lack of energy and courage to launch a career. Neither do they find pride or fulfillment as housewives and mothers. In Ayckbourn's plays, this is seen as "the waste of female potential" caused by the lethargy of the woman figures.

Chekhov portrays two types of unproductive characters: those who do not have any regular occupations and "those whose occupations are meaningless," for they are unable to perform their tasks properly (Senelick, 100). Therefore, the majority of his characters are sterile, regardless whether one has an occupation or not. In *Uncle Vanya*, for instance, the Professor, who has an occupation, is unable to perform his duty effectively, therefore unable to create useful products; and the rest of the characters in the play do not even have any regular jobs. It is argued that the leading figure of sterile individuals in *Uncle Vanya* is the retired professor of fine arts, Serebriakov. The Professor boasts of his academic honors and studies, and "devoting all [his] life to learning," having lived in Moscow for his academic career (*Vanya*, 202). The other characters boast of their "The Herr Professor" as well (*Vanya*, 217). Especially, the Professor's brother-in-law, Uncle Vanya, supported his career by sending him the income of the estate left by the Professor's deceased wife. Vanya "sacrificed himself in the belief that the Professor's career was luminous and deserving support" (Senelick, 88). However, after the Professor's retirement, it becomes obvious now for Vanya that the Professor lacks the necessary intelligence and that his career is not as prolific as it is supposed to be. Vanya expresses both his former devotion to the Professor and his present low opinion of him by these words:

> To us you were a being of a higher order, and we knew your articles by heart. … But now my eyes are opened! I can see it all! You write about art, but you don't understand anything about art! All your works, those works which I used to love, are not worth two pence! You've been deceiving us!
>
> (*Vanya*, 230)

The value of Serebriakov's professorship is reduced to an occupation that has no practical outcome for the others, so "a man supposed so far by Uncle Vanya and others to be an outstanding scholar devoted assiduously to the arts and sciences enlarging the store of human knowledge is now seen to have done nothing, have achieved precious little" (Chakraborty, 68). For Vanya, the Professor lacks the power of creating, but he is the victim of unprolific repetition of what the other men of learning have already said. Such claims of Vanya's assert the Professor's impotence in his occupation:

> [The Professor] has been lecturing and writing about art for exactly twenty-five years, and yet he understands nothing whatever about art. For twenty-five years he has been chewing over other people's ideas about realism, naturalism and all that sort of nonsense; for twenty-five years he has been lecturing and writing about things that intelligent people have known all the time, and stupid people aren't interested in, anyway - in fact, for twenty-five years he's been just wasting time and energy.
>
> (*Vanya*, 191)

It is clear that the Professor represents "the sterile intelligentsia" in Chekhov's drama who are criticized in *The Cherry Orchard*, too: "Nearly all the members of intelligentsia that I know care for nothing, do nothing and are still incapable of work" (*Orchard*, 364).

Confronted with the fact that the Professor's career does not deserve any admiration or support, Vanya "regards his own life as wasted"

(Senelick, 88). For twenty-five years, he has been sending to the Professor the income of the estate to support his career. But the Professor, after his retirement and settlement in the estate, decides to sell the estate in order to lead a more prosperous life with the money. He utters: "We are not made for the country life. But to live in town on the income we're receiving from this estate is also impossible. [...] I suggest we sell it [...] to buy a small villa in Finland" (*Vanya*, 227-228). The Professor's decision of selling the estate proves his parasitic and selfish nature because for twenty-five years he has been depending on the income of the estate like a parasite, but now he wants to sell it for his selfish concerns, paying little attention to others' feelings.

The Professor's wife, Yeliena, is criticized like her husband for being idle and dry. She has no occupation; in fact, she is reluctant to perform any sort of occupation. She is offered many choices of work to do on the estate but Yeliena rejects all of them out of her lack of interest or laziness:

> Sonia: You could help in running the estate, teach children, help to look after the sick. Isn't there plenty to do? For instance, before you and papa came to live here, Uncle Vanya and I used to go to the market ourselves and sell the flour.
> Yeliena: I don't know how to. And I'm not interested.
> (*Vanya*, 217)

Yeliena's rejection of doing nothing on the estate makes her dependent on both Vanya and Sonia, exploiting their energy and efforts. Their family friend, Dr. Astrov, points out her parasitic situation thus: "She does nothing but eat, sleep, go for walks, charm us all by her beauty ... nothing else. She has no responsibilities, other people work for her" (*Vanya*, 210).

Waffles, a landowner reduced to poverty, is the obvious sterile figure in *Uncle Vanya*. He spends most of his time on the estate without doing anything. His life is devoid of any purpose; he is wandering around tuning his guitar most of the time. He lives in the estate as a real parasite —he is "the household hanger-on" (Vitins, 39), but unlike any other characters in Chekhov's drama, he is not oblivious to his parasitic position. He is burdened under the public shame of being a perpetual sponger and a sterile man. He describes how this feeling of shame hurts him with these words: "[A]s I was walking through the village this morning, the shopkeeper shouted after me: 'Hey, you scrounger ... living on other people, you are!' I felt so hurt!" (*Vanya*, 235).

A doctor in a Chekhov play is a regular visitor of the household, who dispenses medical care and wisdom. Dr Astrov in *Uncle Vanya* is such a character; he performs his medical duty with care besides other duties as the reforestation of the land. His counterpart is Dr Chebutykin in *The Three Sisters*, another useless doctor figure in that he does not occupy himself with medical science but instead reads newspaper columns for treatment recipes: "Here is a recipe for falling hair ... two ounces of naphthalene, half-a-bottle of methylated spirit ... dissolve and apply once a day" (*Sisters*, 252). He confesses that he has forgotten his profession —he does not know anything anymore. In his indifference he goes so far as refusing to visit his patients:

> The devil take them all ... all the lot of them! They think I can treat anything just because I'm a doctor, but I know positively nothing at all. I've forgotten everything I used to know. I remember nothing, positively nothing.
>
> (*Sisters*, 298)

The same sterile atmosphere is all-prevailing in *The Cherry Orchard* as in *Uncle Vanya*. The most ironic example to the sterile individuals in *The Cherry Orchard* is Trofimov, a university student at his thirties. Trofimov is an inefficient character since he has not carried his studies to a successful conclusion for years. Being an "eternal student" highlights his unproductivity: "He'll soon be fifty, yet he's still a student" (*Orchard*, 362). Trofimov came to tutor the son of the family, but the son drowned in the river. Nevertheless, since the boy died, Trofimov has been staying on in the estate without anyone to tutor. For six years, he has not looked for another job with another family. Instead, he has been parasitically living off the family for six years. In this respect, he resembles Waffles in *Uncle Vanya*. These two characters are the perfect examples of hangers-on in Chekhov's drama. It is impossible to judge why they live on the estate without being any use to the estate family. When Waffles introduces himself to Yeliena, he is unable to find any word to justify his existence on the estate. Sonia ironically calls him as their great helper on the estate:

> Telyeghin: [...] Ilyia Ilyich Telyeghin, or as some people call me on account of my spotty face, Waffles. [...] I'm now living here on your estate. ... You may have been so kind as to notice that I have dinner with you every day.
> Sonia: Ilyia Ilyich is our helper, our right-hand man.
>
> (*Vanya*, 194)

In *The Cherry Orchard*, the unproductivity of the characters becomes even clearer with the impending sale of the orchard. The estate will be sold to pay the debts of the family, and the auction is going to be held on in a couple of months' time. During this short time, Liubov and Gayev, as the owners of the estate, must figure out a way of saving the estate from the auction. However, they are incapable of generating a positive solution. As sterile individuals, neither landowner has a practical way out to save the cherry orchard from the sale. Since they are impractical and dependent people, they can only think of the idea of sponging on the grandmother for their debts. Unfortunately, the money sent by the grandmother cannot cover their debts. Gayev is expected to devise strategies that bring the orchard back to running order, but funnily enough he has no plan of action. While everyone is worried about the sale of the orchard, Gayev is just "wondering how to retrieve an imaginary billiard shot" (Magarshack, 280). He is a "good-for-nothing" person in the eyes of the other characters (*Orchard*, 352).

The businessman, Lopakhin stands as a doer and achiever among the others in *The Cherry Orchard* as mentioned before. He comes out with practical solutions for the estate. He feels sure he can save the bankrupt estate by convincing Liubov and Gayev to convert the orchard into building lots for cottages. He suggests:

> Your estate is only twenty miles from town, and the rail way line is not far away. Now, if your cherry orchard and the land along the river are divided into plots and leased out for summer residences you'll have a yearly income of at least twenty-five thousand roubles.
>
> (*Orchard*, 343)

When contrasted with the sterility of landowners, Lopakhin's plan can produce a successful conclusion for saving the estate. Furthermore, the landowners will earn more money by renting the cottages according to Lopakhin's plan.

The landowners of the orchard have contributed nothing to the running of the estate, either. They have neglected the family estate, and lived abroad; Liubov first lived in Mentone with her brother and daughter, and then moved to Paris. In their absence, the estate is managed by Varia, Liubov's adopted daughter, and the whole income is sent to them. Liubov and her family members are supported only by this income of the estate, which means they thoroughly depend on Varia and other people's working on the estate. What makes Liubov a selfish parasite is that she has recklessly spent the family fortune without any consideration for Varia and the others, feeding off their energy in the same manner as the Professor wastes the lives of Vanya and Sonia. However, unlike the Professor, Liubov is conscious of the fact that she is dependent on the estate people and that she neglects them for her own sake. Still, her awareness does not lead to any positive and productive plan. She utters: "My poor Varia is feeding everyone on milk soups to economize; the old servants in the kitchen get nothing but dried peas to eat, and here I am, spending money senselessly, I don't know why" (*Orchard*, 357). Both *Uncle Vanya* and *The Cherry Orchard* show that the landowners live off the productivity of the serfs, and they even exploit their close relatives. Trofimov criticizes the Andryeevna family for living their lives at the expense of other people's hard work:

> Your grandfather, your great grandfather and all your forefathers were serf owners —they owned living souls. Don't you see human beings gazing at you from every cherry tree in your orchard, from every leaf and every tree-trunk, don't you hear voices? ... They owned living souls —and it has perverted you all, those who came before you, and you who are living now, so that your mother, your uncle and even you yourself no longer realize that you're living in debt, at other people's expense, at the expense of people you don't admit further than the kitchen.
>
> (*Orchard*, 368)

It is ironic that in a Chekhov play the suggestions for working and producing something come from the individuals who are the most sterile and ignorant of this fact (Senelick, 100), but more ironic than this is the fact that those who are conscious of their sterile and parasitic situation do not have the necessary energy to change this fact. We have seen only Waffles in *Uncle Vanya* and Liubov in *The Cherry Orchard* are conscious of their sterile and parasitic situations. Nevertheless, both characters lack the sufficient strength to improve their situation. Similarly, in *Uncle Vanya*, the Professor and Vanya's mother give emphasis to working and the need for a job, nevertheless, both these characters themselves lack the impetus to fulfill something productive; and similarly, in *The Cherry Orchard*, although Trofimov himself is the most sterile character by being an "eternal student" and an "armchair philosopher," he philosophizes about the importance of working. Trofimov's criticism of Russian people is just a reflection of himself, and stands for the general spirit of *The Cherry Orchard* as well as of *Uncle Vanya*:

> We ought to —just work. [...] Humanity is perpetually advancing, always seeking to perfect its own powers. One day all the things that are beyond our grasp at present are going to fall

within our reach, only to achieve this we've got to work with all our might, to help the people who are seeking after truth. Here, in Russia, very few people have started to work so far. Nearly all the members of the intelligentsia that I know care for nothing, do nothing and are still incapable of work. They call themselves 'intelligentsia', but they still talk contemptuously to their servants, they treat the peasants as if they were animals, they study without achieving anything, they don't read anything serious, they just do nothing.

(*Orchard*, 363-364)

In Ayckbourn drama the presentation of the unproductive characters is likened to Chekhovian portrayal of sterile individuals. Ayckbourn's men and women are unable to produce anything on their own, and like those of Chekhov they are supported by other characters in turn. Ayckbourn presents in *Henceforward* a pivotal character who has a job but is still sterile, especially like Chekhov's Professor of arts in *Uncle Vanya*. Jerome, in *Henceforward*, lives alone in a flat, shut out from his family and the rest of the society, surrounded by his computers. He is an artist who composes music for TV advertisements. He seems to be a man of creative talent like the Professor —he sees himself as a famous composer who wrote the popular music for an advertisement which was shown "ten times a night, every night for about eight months" (*Henceforward*, 26). Nonetheless, beneath the superficial creativity of Jerome, he is an unfruitful person in his profession because he is solely dependent on the voices of other people to produce his so-called masterpiece. Furthermore, he has been incapable of producing any meaningful and practical piece of music for years. In this respect, Jerome's efforts to compose original pieces are as futile as that of the Professor in his academic studies. The works of both these men of creative talent signify nothing to the other people around them.

Jerome aspires "to express the feeling of love in an abstract musical form" (*Henceforward*, 39). He tries to convey this feeling mechanically by the help of his hi-tech digital keyboards but he is unskilled to bring about the sound of love, for "in human terms, [he] is incapable of understanding it" (Billington, 196). Jerome indicates that it is impossible for him to produce mechanically the feeling of love: "I know what I want to say. It is how to say it. I haven't got the sound, I haven't heard it" (*Henceforward*, 39). As Billington states, Jerome is not capable of recognizing any real human feeling, therefore, he is impotent in composing the sound of genuine love (196).

In Chekhov's plays the sterile individuals depend on other people close to them when they themselves are inadequate as depicted in *Uncle Vanya* and *The Cherry Orchard*. Ayckbourn's drama, too, presents dependent figures because they are inert characters. It dramatizes wives that depend on their husbands not only for living but also for their own happiness, or for any other matter: "I never read the papers. I haven't read a paper since I married. I rely on Sven [her husband] to tell me if there's a war broken out" (*Apart*, 153). Ayckbourn's dependent figures parasitically feed off the others' lives and energy as Chekhov's people do. Similarly, when Jerome himself is deprived of the capacity to create something on his own, he is "parasitically feeding off the lives, the emotions and needs of those closest to him" (Billington, 194). In order to produce his works of creation, he entirely depends on the emotions of other people near and dear to him. He records his wife's and daughter's voices without their permission and uses these voices by means of his digital keyboards. For his famous music, Jerome used his daughter's natural voice. In the same manner, he records Zoë's voice while they are making love, and her reaction to that puts forward Jerome's despicable side of being a scrounger:

> You recorded that while we were —? [...] I don't believe it. You mean, while we were making love you just calmly lent out of bed and switched on a tape recorder? [...] never known anything so sick in my life ... it is disgusting.
> (*Henceforward*, 48, 50)

Jerome's way of making compositions completely supported by the feelings of others brings to mind the parasitic life style of Chekhov's Professor.

His exploitation of other people runs even to the extent of making use of the privacy of his wife, daughter, and finally Zoë. She complains: "My God, did you do this sort of thing to your wife? To your daughter? [...] I mean, there is such a thing as basic privacy ... just to record someone without even ..." (*Henceforward*, 49-50).

Most of Ayckbourn's female characters lead a parasitic life which resembles the life style of Chekhov's characters. In an Ayckbourn play, women characters' laziness and their lack of energy and courage to do something with themselves and with their lives are given as the main reasons for the women characters' being dependent individuals. In *Woman in Mind*, Ayckbourn portrays Susan as a dependent character. Susan is reflected as a lazy and idle figure who does not have a proper job that can save her from idleness but has never thought of carving a career for herself either. The reader is given the clue of the fact that in her early marriage days Susan regarded the housework and child upbringing as her proper job; however, it becomes certain from her bitter complaining that she now suffers from the lack of a proper job. Nevertheless, despite her complaining of having no job, she does not have the least inclination and strength to go out and find one. Throughout the play, the on-stage action takes place in "Susan's garden and beyond," and during the whole play, Susan never goes into the house. She is seen living in her garden idly without doing any work; still, the garden is untidy and the flowers are not looked after properly. Her husband, Gerald, now and then asks ironically: "Is that bush dead? It looks dead from here" (*Mind*, 10). Her sister-in-law, Muriel, too, complains about the untidiness of the garden: "This garden could do with a tidy, couldn't it? That bush is dead" (*Mind*, 14). Yet, Susan, who spends all her time in the garden, is not interested in looking after it. Gerald, the insensitive husband that he is, makes it clear that Susan is always sleeping and daydreaming in the garden. Her laziness is emphasized by Gerald when he criticizes Susan for this with a satirical tone: "You sleep all day ... There is a school of thought that believes that sleep is for the night. You seem to be out to disapprove them" (*Mind*, 10).

During the play, Susan is never seen while she is doing any kind of housework, either. Even if she is inside at home, we can understand that Susan's idleness would continue since she admits that she "watch[es] far too much television" all the time (*Mind*, 22). Thus, it is her sister-in-law who is supposed to be in charge of running the house, cooking and serving. Susan depends on her sister-in-law to manage the household. Muriel makes coffee for the guests, sets the table for meals, and cleans the kitchen. Even when Susan's son returns home after a long period of time, the lunch to celebrate his homecoming is again cooked by Muriel, although Gerald reminds Susan many times to prepare the meal. Muriel complains: "she'd have made some herself by now, rather than leaving it to me" (*Mind*, 14). Ironically, Susan denies her help and thinks that she herself does every kind of work, like a hard working housewife. When Susan lists to Gerald the housework she is supposed to be doing, the reader knows that it is impossible to do all this and at the same time doze off in the garden or watch too much television. She complains: "I run this house. I do all the cooking, the bulk of the washing up, *all* the laundry- including Muriel's —I cope with the sheer boring slog of tidying up after both of you, day after day, I make the beds" (*Mind*, 11). However, Gerald reminds Susan and the reader with a satirical tone that in fact not Susan but Muriel works hard, and Susan depends on her as a sponger:

> Susan: I work extremely hard, Gerald, and you know it. I help you whenever I'm able. I run this house for you —
> Gerald: With the help of my sister, you do
>
> (*Mind*, 11)

When Susan fails with her real family, she has hallucinations of a fantasy family to compensate for this failure. The members of her fantasy family are just the opposite of her real family members. It is seen that only Susan remains the same: she is still a hanger-on even in her hallucinations. She wants both of her families to serve her constantly, and her fantasy husband is always around ready to satisfy Susan's desires. It can be said that she exploits both her families with her idleness and indolence.

Ayckbourn, after Chekhov, portrays "good for nothing" characters like Chekhov's Gayev in *The Cherry Orchard*. Sven is reflected as a good for nothing man in Ayckbourn's *Joking Apart*. He is cramped in the company. He always complains that his partner Richard has taken the control and that he is never given any chance to decide and to act, thereby being reduced to impotency —"reduced to nothing more than a piece of glorified office furniture" (*Apart*, 34). Another partner Brian, too, is restrained in managing the company by Richard's control over everything. He is always seen helping Richard; he acts according to what Richard tells him to do. The sterile and parasitic people of Chekhov and Ayckbourn theatre, in conclusion, are superfluous characters. The overall effect of their inertia makes them nonentities living on earth for no purpose and benefit for mankind. They signify nothing for the others; they are like useless and unneeded machines as Ayckbourn dramatizes in *Henceforward*. After the departure of his wife and daughter, Jerome now lives with an android which he repaired and improved. It is a Nan 300F model android programmed to look after children. However, such a nanny is unskilled to take care of children properly as "one of them ... put a baby in a microwave oven" (*Henceforward*, 89). Besides, there is no child around. Nan can be compared to Chekhov's Trofimov on the ground that Trofimov is a tutor but there is no one in *The Cherry Orchard* for him to tutor, so he becomes redundant. Similarly, Nan is superfluous because she is unfulfilled. Nan, the android, in *Henceforward* is the symbolic representation of man's sterility and man's craving to find fulfillment:

> Wandering about, looking for a child to look after. Unfulfilled, almost. In so far as a machine can be unfulfilled, of course. I suppose no more so than, say, a coffee grinder that can't find any beans to grind could be described as unfulfilled. [...] Well, there's more to her than a coffee grinder.
>
> (*Henceforward*, 25)

Pervading Atmosphere

The pervading atmosphere in Chekhov's plays is that of the drowsy and sterile one, which is the instrument for evoking the mood of inertia in both the characters and the audience. This mood is conveyed through some certain images and symbolic actions or non-actions of the characters. They fall asleep and yawn all the time, and regularly refer to their ailments, which physically hamper the characters, highlight their inactivity, and create the pervading aura of inertia. In a Chekhov play, the innately inert characters become paralyzed men and women leading the same static life continuously, which imbues the aura of the play with inaction rather than action. Chekhov describes *The Seagull* as a play which contains "a lot of talk about literature, not much action, tons of love." In Chekhov's other plays, there is obviously "not much action," either, except idle gossip, eating, drinking, vain dreams of happiness, endless tea and vodka. The setting for this sterile atmosphere is always a country estate which the characters regard as the center of paralysis. The characters either sip their tea or vodka in the estate gardens idly contemplating life, people and vague plans.

Chekhov opens his plays by some symbolic actions and dialogues of his characters, and by certain images to create a "numbing atmosphere" in the plays (Senelick, 95). *The Cherry Orchard* opens with the yawning and stretching of Lopakhin. He informs the audience that he "came here on purpose to go to the station and meet them [Andryeevna family] —and then overslept! ... Drop off to sleep in the chair" (*Orchard*, 333). Act III of *The Cherry Orchard* opens with Pishchik's talk but in the middle of his talk he all of a sudden "falls asleep and snores" (*Orchard*, 370). A. R. Kugel points out that "the inhabitants of *The Cherry Orchard* live, as if half asleep, spectrally" (qtd. in Senelick, 126). Any Chekhov play, according to Desmond McCarthy, establishes "an atmosphere of sighs and yawns" (qtd. in Magarshack, 18).

The references to some ailments of the characters contribute to the creation of the same atmosphere. In *Uncle Vanya*, the lifeless and heavy mood is supplied by the Professor's difficulty to move because of his rheumatism. His ailment causes painful swellings in the joints of his knees, which sometimes impairs his movement. The pain in his legs is unbearable as he states: "I dozed off just now and I dreamt that my left leg didn't belong to me. I was woken up by an agonizing pain. No, it's not gout; it's more like rheumatism" (*Vanya*, 201). In *The Cherry Orchard*, likewise, Pishchik suffers from gout that hinders his movement (*Orchard*, 349). These ailments that physically cripple the characters visually contribute to the ineptness and weariness of the characters. Chekhov's characters, as a result, become death-like individuals. The dramatist gives the ghostly atmosphere of his plays through the symbols of mourning; in the opening scene of *The Seagull*, "Masha's appearance in her black dress at once strikes the note that will be characteristic of the whole play" (Magarshack, 162). The same morbid atmosphere prevails in the opening scene of *The Three Sisters*. Olga opens the play with her mourning words: "It's exactly a year ago that Father died" (*Sisters*, 249); therefore, she creates the ghostly atmosphere of the play. This mood has a pressing effect on the characters. Olga is the first one affected by the deadening mood of the play. She complains of losing her energy: "I seem to have the thoughts of someone quite old. Honestly, I've been feeling as if my strength and youth were running out of me drop by drop" (*Sisters*, 250).

Ayckbourn's mastery of mood and situation is descended from Chekhov. He himself identifies a Chekhovian phase in the "plays where nothing much happens, like *Absent Friends* and *Just Between Ourselves*" (*The Economist*, 87). In Ayckbourn's plays, there is little action on the stage, which symbolically brings his characters' lethargy to the foreground, and establishes his plays' all-pervasive sterile atmosphere. Ayckbourn, also, realizes that the general atmosphere of the play complements the mood of the characters. However, he does not present them in a "gloomy" atmosphere. His characters move about in a seemingly "jolly" set up, behind which they are utterly miserable. They are constantly in and out of various parties to celebrate an occasion. The happy atmosphere, though, is just pretence to emphasize by contrast the characters' unhappiness. In *Season's Greetings*, the action takes place on Christmas Eve, Christmas Day, and on Boxing Day. Likewise, the characters in *Just Between Ourselves* come together to celebrate each other's birthday; in Act I, it is Dennis's birthday celebrated, and in Act II, it is Marjories's and Neil's. In *Joking Apart* a garden party is held and all the characters seem to be entertaining gaily with fireworks. Nevertheless, the characters' grieves are still discernable although the setting is that of a celebration nearly in most of Ayckbourn's plays. Instead of Chekhovian country life, Ayckbourn reflects suburban life as the center of boredom and paralysis, and Chekhovian estate gardens give their places to the private gardens where the characters spend all their time doing nothing except endless chatter —"as soon as you arrive here it's food, drink, food, drink" (*Apart*, 162).

FRUSTRATION

Dissatisfaction is one of the character traits that Ayckbourn shares with Chekhov to portray his dramatis personae as people discontent with their lives and unhappy without any easily discernable reason. Characters of both dramatists pursue different walks of life for the single aim of happiness. They may go in for different things: art, literature, fame, business, love or marriage. However, they cannot realize their dreams of happiness, and frustration mars their contentment. Both Chekhov and Ayckbourn draw their characters as frustrated individuals who can never attain a real fulfillment because their hopes, desires and aims are ruined by the forces that come between the characters and their dreams.

In Chekhov's drama, characters are by no means able to bring their wishes to completion or reach their aims. His characters have great ambitions; yet, their ambitions are defeated by frustrating forces. Thus, they are proved to be incapable of achieving happiness. *The Seagull* dramatizes people complaining of unhappiness —certain dissatisfaction with life — though they have almost everything. Masha opens the play with her complaints about her discontentment but she is unable to find any sufficient reason for this; she is unhappy but this is not due to any lack of health or wealth as understood from the below quotation from the play:

> Medviedenko: Why do you always wear black?
> Masha: I'm in mourning for my life. I'm unhappy.
> Medviedenko: But why? (Meditatively) I can't understand it. You're in good health. Your father isn't rich, but he's comfortably off. [...]
> Masha: It isn't money that matters. Even a pauper can be happy.
> (*Seagull*, 119)

The principal theme of Chekhov's *The Three Sisters*, too, is the frustration of the sisters. In the opening scene, they are full of hopes for their future lives. Their primary expectation is to return to Moscow, where they believe life would be generous to make them all successful. The three sisters spent their early youth in Moscow and had good education there, so the place is the scene of their happiest memories. They expect their brother Andrey will be a professor in Moscow and bring them back to this city, relieving them from the boredom of the country life. However, the sisters are driven away from their hopes and happiness as their brother Andrey, who is supposed to become a scholar in Moscow, marries a local country girl and settles in the very same town they have already been living, quitting the idea of becoming a professor. Therefore, their monotonous life continues and it dashes the sisters' wishful thinking. Symbolizing their disillusionment, Moscow becomes "a source of frustration and unhappiness" for the three sisters (Valency, 186).

Chekhov's characters experience frustration in every aspect of their lives. The dramatist entangles his characters in love affairs to exploit the theme of frustration. Thomas A. Eekman claims: "Frustration and human failure are themes that Chekhov preferred to treat in the sphere of conjugal love" (145). His four full-length plays dramatize love affairs that offer no union for the lovers, and several affairs of unrequited love. Chekhov's characters search for their happiness as they go after their lovers; however, they face bitter frustration when their love is not reciprocated or when it cannot end in marriage. In *The Seagull*, the seagull becomes the symbolization of Chekhov's characters' frustration in that when Konstantin's love for Nina goes unresponded, he kills the bird to warn that his end is going to be the same if she does not respond to her love. In *Uncle Vanya*, Sonia's frustration is caused by her unrequited love for Astrov. She loves the country doctor, and she identifies herself with his ideas and great plans for the future. For Sonia, Astrov is the embodiment of great ideas and she desires to be united with these ideas, thereby planning to seize happiness since these are her objectives as well. Yet, "Sonya's attempt at happiness with Astrov is also frustrated" (Bordinat, 56). When her love is rejected, Sonia's aspiration for such a union is ruined. Masha of *The Three Sisters* is married to a narrow-minded schoolteacher, Fiodor Ilyich. She is unhappy with her marriage and she tries to find happiness with her secret love affair with The Battery Commander Vershinin. He stands as the embodiment of freedom that Masha yearns for, and she sees her love affair as an escape for freedom. Nevertheless, their love affair offers no union for them. Vershinin leaves the country with the battery, and Masha has to return to her husband, frustrated and resigned to an unhappy marriage.

Ayckbourn, on the other hand, uses marital relations to exploit the theme of dissatisfaction in his plays, creating his recurrent theme of "marital discontent". His characters cannot grasp happiness and they believe that their marital commitments are the very cause of their disillusionment. Whenever they find that they have not carried out their goals or have gone off their dreams, they accuse their husbands or wives, and even their children, as the source of their frustration. For instance, in Pam and Neil's marriage in *Just Between Ourselves*, there is no well-adjusted, happy husband-wife relationship. Neil is seen as a weak and impotent husband. Thus, Pam thinks he does not have the capacity to satisfy her emotional and "sexual" desires. Between the lines, Neil gives clues of this negligence:

> Neil: At night time. I wake up and she's grabbing on to me. Digging in with her fingernails, you know …
> Dennis: That's probably what's wrong with your shoulder.
> Neil: And scratching —I've got a terrible scratch mark.
> Dennis: Well, fancy that. She doesn't look the sort.

> Neil: No.
> Dennis: What do you do?
> Neil: Well, I say like —lay off, will you. I'm trying to get to sleep. I mean, it's about four in the morning she starts this.
> Dennis: You need your sleep.
> Neil: I do. I need eight hours.
>
> *(Ourselves*, 40)

Pam believes that Neil is "systematically destroying [her]" by ignoring her desires (*Ourselves*, 57). She is tied to the house to look after her son and her ill mother, having quitted her job for her marriage. She has the feeling that she is left alone at home and finally accuses Neil for this negligence. She states: "You have left me with the running of the house entirely. You have left me to bring up your child and you have left me to nurse mother on my own" (*Ourselves*, 51). Therefore, as the above quotation makes clear, she strongly believes that it is Neil who destroyed her yearnings.

In *Absent Friends*, Diana sees her marriage with Paul as the sole cause responsible for her failure to attain her dream. After quarreling with Paul, Diana, "in a trance of her own," begins a moving monologue, making her previous strong yearning public: "I had this burning ambition, you see, to join the Canadian Royal Mounted Police" (*Friends*, 41). Her desire has not been realized owing to the prejudice of the society. She is told: "Little girls don't join the Mounted police. Little girls do nice things like typing and knitting and nursing and having babies" (*Friends*, 41). Her sobs become even louder and louder till everyone is stunned. Paul comes down to help Diana but she fights him away. She now believes that it is her marriage that has deprived her of her wishes, not the bias of the society. However, the reader can understand that "she has sacrificed her own desires to fulfill the expectations of the society," as Youssef explains the gist of the matter (58). Frustrated and disappointed, Diana marries Paul instead of joining the Mounted Police. She utters:

> So I married Paul instead. Because they refused to let me join the Mounted Police. I married him because he kept asking me.

And because people kept saying that it would be a much nicer thing to do than —and so I did. And I learnt my typing and I had my babies and I looked after them for as long as they'd let me and then suddenly I realized I'd been doing all the wrong things. They'd been wrong telling me to marry Paul and have babies, if they're not even going to let you keep them and I should have joined the Mounted Police, that's what I should have done.

(*Friends*, 41)

Chekhov's characters, as it is seen, miserably seek for their happiness as they follow their unattainable loves. They identify themselves with their lovers; nonetheless, they can never fulfill their ideals or reach happiness through their love affairs since they can never attain either a well-balanced relation or a union in their love affairs. Ayckbourn's characters, on the other hand, are already married, but cannot reach happiness within their marriages. They think their marital commitments hinder them from realizing their ideals. "Male insensitivity" in Ayckbourn's plays is generally interpreted as the single reason for the lack of mutual understanding in marriages depicted by the dramatist and for the mental collapse of his women characters. With regard to *Just Between Ourselves*, for instance, it is argued that Ayckbourn "even wrote a particularly abrasive comedy about a woman driven into a state of catatonia by an uncomprehending husband" (Billington, 181). However, Ayckbourn never puts forward openly that only male characters as insensitive husbands are responsible for the female dissatisfaction in his theatre. He objectively presents both male and female characters in his plays, which makes women characters equally responsible for the disillusionment in their marriages. With the aim of clarifying additional reasons for women characters' dissatisfaction in Ayckbourn drama, it is argued that Ayckbourn's women characters are dissatisfied due to the loss of a stable identity. Felicia Hardison Londré in her essay entitled "Ayckbourn's Women" regards female dissatisfaction in Ayckbourn's plays as the result of women characters' inability to construct a stable identity for themselves (87). In the light of her argument, two of Ayckbourn's plays, *Just Between Ourselves* and *Woman in Mind*, can be explored here in terms of female dissatisfaction. Vera and Pam in *Just Between Ourselves* and Susan, the pivotal figure of *Woman in Mind*, are incapable of defining their roles. The primary function for the three women characters that helps define their roles is their marriages in both *Just Between Ourselves* and *Woman in Mind* because, as it is claimed by Londré, "the marital tie serves as the major defining feature" of the roles of female figures in Ayckbourn drama (88). However, Ayckbourn's women characters fail to define themselves as wives since they regard themselves as the victims of unhappy marriages.

The central married couple in *Just Between Ourselves* is Vera and Dennis. Vera sees herself as the victim of an unhappy marriage because she believes she is constantly neglected by her husband who spends most of his time in his garage "disastrously tinkering at various do-it-yourself projects" (Billington, 111) and paying little attention to the outer world. For Vera, this is the utter negligence of Dennis; they supposedly share the same household but Vera feels lonely. She says: "You never seem to be here, Dennis […] you're out here, aren't you? […] Most of the time" (*Ourselves*, 53). Vera's unhappiness and disillusionment with her marriage are caused by emotional neglect, and the lack of sharing the same house with her husband performs the function of a deterrent for Vera's defining her role as a housewife. Being all alone with her mother-in-law at home, Vera cannot figure out the aim and the importance of her role as a wife, and she begins to question this: "I spend all day trying to make [home] nice. […] I mean, what is the point of my […] doing everything? I mean, what is the point?" (*Ourselves*, 53). As a result, finding no point in making her home nice for a husband who passes most of his time in the garage, Vera gradually loses the defining function of the role of a wife in marriage. Similarly, Pam's aspiration to settle her identity with her marital tie is just an utter failure like that of Vera as she also lacks a happy husband-wife relationship in her marriage which would help Pam to define her identity as Neil's wife. We have seen that she deems that Neil is the sole cause of her shattered aspirations. Describing herself "unfulfilled, frustrated," she comes to be one of the desperate housewives of Ayckbourn's theatre (*Ourselves*, 56).

In *Woman in Mind*, Susan, likewise, is seen to be suffering from an uncomprehending husband, Gerald, who seems to be failing to care for her. As in Vera's and Pam's case, Susan regards herself as the neglected woman in the house, and like the other women characters in Ayckbourn's plays, she endeavors to find a proper role in her marriage. Nonetheless, the lack of understanding and sharing between husband and wife hinders Susan in identifying herself with the wife-role in a marriage:

> I don't know what my role is these days. I don't any longer know what I'm supposed to be doing. I used to be a wife. I used to be mother. And I loved it. People said, "Oh, don't you long to get out and do a proper job?" And I'd say, "No thanks, this is a proper job, thank you. Mind your own business." But now it isn't any more.
>
> (*Mind*, 11)

Vera's attempts in *Just Between Ourselves* and Susan's in *Woman in Mind* to define their roles as happy wives are further obstructed by the intrusion of a third person into their marriages. Vera's would-be happy marriage is deterred by the intrusion of her mother-in-law, Marjorie, into her marriage. Dennis's mother lives together with Vera and Dennis, and she wants to be the domineering member of the family; she is "determined to maintain her hold over her son" (Billington, 111). For her, Dennis is still her child who needs the care of a mother. Accordingly, she claims that Vera is inadequate as a wife to cherish the necessary care for Dennis. Her claim to Vera's role as a wife is manifest particularly when Vera does not make a cake for Dennis's birthday party. She authoritatively states that she has always made Dennis's cake: "Ever since he was a little boy, he's always had his cake. Even when your father was dying, Dennis, I still made your cake" (*Ourselves*, 44). By uttering this, she implies Vera's inadequacy as a wife. In a satirical voice, she says: "I think the least you could have done, Vera, is to make him a cake. It was really thoughtless to forget"

(*Ourselves*, 45). Therefore, Marjorie is depicted as Vera's rival who wants to take over her role as a housewife, "to break up her home" (*Ourselves*, 59). Before her final silence resulted from her catatonic situation, Vera screams this fact at her mother-in-law: "You have always hated me. You have always wanted my home" (*Ourselves*, 59). Nonetheless, the mother-in-law succeeds in the end in gaining Vera's home and undertaking her role as a housewife, a claim which obstructs Vera's attempts to define herself as housewife. When Marjorie achieves this claim, Vera, having no self-definition as a housewife, is drowned into a catatonic situation. At the end of the play, she is seen outside the house sitting silently in the garden in "a cold clear morning" (*Ourselves*, 61), leaving her home to her mother-in-law. At last, Dennis's mother is in charge of house managing and she is full of joy with Vera's being silent: "That's better. Now you just sit there quietly. You have no need to worry, do you hear? Dennis is being taken good care of. I'll see to him. You just look after yourself" (*Ourselves*, 62). She is characterized as the "domineering mother who only achieves happiness when Vera is reduced to silence and she can resume her role as surrogate-wife" (Billington, 114).

In *Woman in Mind*, Susan has to share her home with her sister-in-law, Muriel. Gerald's sister is the intruder of Susan and Gerald's marriage in that she has been living together with them after her husband's death. Although Muriel is unable to do any housework properly, she seems to be completely in charge of running the house. Susan wants to see it as her role to do all housework but she is intruded in this by her sister-in-law, thereby being intruded in defining herself as a housewife as well. It is safe to say that Muriel manages to take the responsibility of the household on herself like Marjorie in *Just Between Ourselves*, and thus Susan feels herself useless, without a role as a wife, as a mother, and even as a housewife.

Ayckbourn's married women are also defined by their social roles as "career women" since beyond their marriages and beyond house management, women characters' office jobs can serve as another self-defining function of their roles (Londré, 94). The lack of any proper job of female characters in Ayckbourn's plays deprives them from a social self-definition. The women characters in both plays under discussion cannot define themselves by their jobs since they do not have any profession of their own. The two women of *Just Between Ourselves*, Vera and Pam point out that they had to leave their jobs after their marriages, which annoys both women now (*Ourselves*, 37). The two women's constant reminiscences about their old jobs can be taken as a sign indicating the fact that they long for their identities as working women. When they used to have a proper profession, Vera and Pam must have been able to reach a self-definition as "career women". However, when they stop working after their marriages, the defining function of an office job disappears together with it.

Susan in *Woman in Mind* is another Ayckbourn woman who cannot fix her role as a working woman. It is indicated in the play that she has never had a job, and she has seen her housework as a proper job for her. She states that in her early marriage days she treated the housework and child upbringing as her proper job. Nevertheless, because she is dissatisfied with her identity as a housewife, Susan does not regard it as a proper job any more (*Mind*, 11). She aspires to be a working woman and to define her role with the profession she would be doing.

The loss of self-definition and dissatisfaction with their present roles, when combined with their uncomprehending husbands, bring the women characters in both plays to the brick of mental breakdown. Pam finds herself imitating to drive Dennis's car in the garage. She is described as suffering from "car sick" (*Ourselves*, 58). For Vera, the case is much harsher than being a "car sick". When she fails to assert her identity in any way and especially when she leaves her home to her mother-in-law, Vera is driven into a mental collapse. The play ends when she is in a state of catatonia sitting silently in the garden in a cold January day. Likewise, Susan's world of hallucinations comes to its inevitable ruin for her when the real and fantasy families merge in her imagination. In the final scene of the play, Susan is in a schizophrenic state uttering totally meaningless words, and it is pointed out in the stage direction that "she is starting to be lit now by the reflection of an ambulance's blue flashing light" (*Mind*, 61).

In Ayckbourn plays, marriage becomes a destructive institution with its dissatisfaction and disillusionment on both sides, on husbands and wives. Ayckbourn himself, like his characters, sees marriage as a trap. In his conversations with Ian Watson, he reveals his reaction to marriage as: "In general, I don't think people were meant to live with each other for too long. [...] As soon as people feel that they are married, there is sense of entrapment" (Watson, 75). Both female and male characters in Ayckbourn theatre experience this feeling of entrapment within their marriages; and also the marital disharmony is the characteristic feature of the marriages in the writer's plays, leading to a lack of mutual understanding between the couples. The dissatisfaction of male characters in the playwright's theatre can be regarded to be the outcome of this entrapment in marriage. Ayckbourn's male characters are exposed to the necessity of satisfying their wives' never-ending demands in marriage who become self-centered characters particularly when they are at the brick of schizophrenia. Neil in *Just Between Ourselves* is the only person to realize that husbands and wives "both expect things from each other. Things that the other one is not prepared to give ... to the other one" (*Ourselves*, 47). Ayckbourn's male characters, therefore, are portrayed as equally miserable, unhappy husbands as his female characters, suffering the same dissatisfaction in their marriages as do their wives. Whereas the marital disharmony and the dissatisfaction of female characters push them into the state of schizophrenia in both plays, the male characters accomplish to escape from this entrapment and dissatisfaction within marriage by guarding their selves with effective defense mechanism which protects them psychologically from mental collapse by denial, conversion, and repression of the problems, and with the help of their hobby-like jobs. These are unimportant jobs of male characters, just passing their time by doing unnecessary things, because in the plays it is seen that Dennis never manages to mend anything or Gerald cannot complete his book. Nevertheless, Ayckbourn's male figures in both plays abort the imprisonment of marriage-trap in this way through escaping into their separate worlds. Ayckbourn's male characters are not perpetual-happy husbands; still, they seem to be strong figures because they are, as Gerald points out in *Woman in Mind*, "just better at hiding these things," or they are, as Dennis indicates in *Just Between Ourselves*, "immune to marriage".

In Ayckbourn marriages, women hide themselves behind the idea of "male insensitivity," indicating that it is always the husband who neglects his wife in a marriage. Ayckbourn's female characters are seen as "the innocent victims —the Veras and the Pams" (White, 94). Studies on Ayckbourn drama focus to a considerable extent on the fact that it is entirely male insensitivity that causes their wives' mental injury. However, it is discussed here that in *Just Between Ourselves* and *Woman in Mind*, the female characters are driven into mental breakdown additionally when they are unable to define their roles and fix their identities. Furthermore, it is depicted in the two plays analyzed that Ayckbourn's dissatisfied women characters give rise to male dissatisfaction within their marriages as well. Male characters are anatomized as the unhappy husbands who are expected to satisfy their wives' all wishes. Against all these that push females into mental collapse, male characters try to protect their selves with effective and proper psychological reactions; and they are successful in this. The dissatisfaction with marriage that causes female characters' mental breakdown does not seem to make any harm to Ayckbourn's men, the Dennises and the Geralds.

Frustrating Forces

Chekhov's and Ayckbourn's men and women are seemingly hampered by multiple outside forces; their social environment, their fellowmen, the circumstances surrounding them and their marital ties may deprive them from reaching happiness. For the three sisters, for example, as mentioned before, their happiness is marred by Andrey, and Andrey's, in turn, by his marriage. He is identified with his ambition for being a professor, but at the end he proves to be unable to accomplish this; and he believes that his marriage is the only reason for his frustration. Likewise, for Diana and Pam it is their marriages that thwart their ambition. Marital tie generally stands as an outside frustrating force for Ayckbourn's characters. Nevertheless, these outside forces are the excuses both Chekhov's and Ayckbourn's characters give for their own incapability of realizing their objectives. The main cause of their frustration is the characters themselves. Their own inertia is seen as the underlying and never changing force that prevents them from accomplishing their aims. Trying to find out the reason behind the disillusionment and dissatisfaction that Chekhov's characters suffer from, Oscar G. Brockett indicates that "the characters long for happiness and wish to live useful and full lives, but they are constantly thwarted by […] their own personalities" (323). The passive nature and unwillingness of Chekhov's and Ayckbourn's characters are more instrumental than the outside elements, because they easily accept what befalls them and it never occurs to inept individuals to struggle with these outside forces. Furthermore, they themselves do nothing to activate their objectives. They have wishful thinking but no action; they wait for a miracle that will satisfy their desires and make them happy.

In Chekhov's *The Three Sisters*, Andrey's staying in the country is the excuse that the sisters hide their own ineptitude behind. It never occurs to them that they can leave the country and go to Moscow with or without the help of Andrey. "Almost from the play's première, critics wondered what was stopping Prozorovs [the sisters] from buying a ticket to the big city," asks Laurence Senelick (107). There is, actually, no other force that blocks the sisters' aim but their own lethargic nature. What circumvents them is their stagnation, so their dissatisfaction is said to be of their making: "*Three Sisters* does not try to show how three gifted women were defeated by a philistine environment, but rather that their unhappiness is their own making" (Senelick, 110). In *The Seagull*, on the other hand, Konstantin wants to be a well-known writer and he is on the way of becoming one with his play for the stage. What he needs is his mother's approval as a successful actress. However, it is seen that "the young man meets with failure in every direction: his play is scoffed at by his mother" (Senelick, 70). She degrades Konstantin's plans by her bitter criticism of his work. His low self-esteem and fragile courage make him accept defeat easily. Therefore, his aspiration of becoming a playwright goes unfulfilled. Consequently, "frustrated and confused, [Konstantin] destroys his manuscripts and shoots himself, this time successfully" (Senelick, 74).

In Ayckbourn's plays, similarly, it is the characters' apathetic nature that mars their happiness. His characters let their yearnings be ruined primarily by their own inertia. In *Woman in Mind*, Susan, for instance, does nothing to reach her aims, therefore satisfaction; she always demands that people around her make her happy. In her case, the miracle which is supposed to bring happiness is her fantasy family. She believes that her fantasy husband is such a wonder that he is capable of meeting Susan's every demand. Pam and Vera in *Just Between Ourselves* quitted their jobs after their marriages and for their marriages since their "priorities change" (*Ourselves*, 37). The two women now think that their loss of a career is caused by the commitments, duties and changes which marriage life demands of them. However, it is an excuse which hides their lack of energy since "there's nothing to stop [them]. If [they] really want to," as Pam encourages Vera (*Ourselves*, 38)

Fantasy Worlds

When frustrated characters realize that they cannot cope with disillusioned life, they revert to a fantasy. In Chekhov's *Uncle Vanya*, Astrov claims, "[w]hen people have no real life, they live on their illusions" (*Vanya*, 209). Fantasy is merely a wish-fulfilling activity, compensating for lack of achievement, and "wish fulfilling fantasies [...] are divorced from reality" (Coleman, 88). It means that the characters in both writers' plays distort bitter realities according to their wishes and thus they create a relatively smoother world that they can easily cope with than the actual world. This is, of course, an escape from facing realities by burying themselves into a fantasy world with a distorted perception of reality. Chekhov's and Ayckbourn's characters systematically reorganize and reinterpret reality to satisfy their wishes, so they build up an alternative reality.

Chekhov's characters express their wishes about the future but those wishes are, according to Laurence Senelick, "[u]topian alternatives to the dreary provincial life" (106). They always complain about country boredom and hope to get rid of this country life, but Senelick regards these hopes utopian, unattainable desires, giving his reason that "the men who formulate them are ineffectual, with no chance of realizing their 'thick-coming fancies'" (106); that is, the complaints and wishes of Chekhov's characters remain as fancies since the characters are unwilling and unable to realize them. In *The Three Sisters*, when the sisters get disillusioned by their actual country life which offers them no proper occupation according to their talents, no chance to use their foreign languages and finally no happy marriage or love affair, they begin to dream of Moscow as a utopian place where they would feel much happier. None of the sisters is able to catch any satisfaction in their provincial life because they are not aware that they can find the contentment they look for in the country as well. When Masha utters, "knowing three languages in a town like this is an unnecessary luxury [...] a sort of useless encumbrance" (*Sisters*, 263), Vershinin's reply to her asserts that even in the country one can still make use of his knowledge and get satisfaction: "It seems to me that there's no place on earth, however dull and depressing it may be; where intelligence and education can be useless" (*Sisters*, 263). Being ineffectual to formulate a way of using their talents, the sisters hold that they could live useful if they were in Moscow: "To Moscow, to Moscow!" The city is a dream world for them, "somewhere over the rainbow, just out of sight" where they believe they would find happiness (Senelick, 107). The sisters create an alternative world with Moscow by distorting the reality that they live useless.

Chekhov's characters alter the present realities by talking endlessly about the promising future and reminiscing about the happy past: "Aware of their failings, these people reach out for the meaning for their sufferings and on occasion dream of a glorious and distant future which would compensate for their wasted lives" (Yarmolinsky, 20). They create a dream world in the same manner with a nostalgic yearning for the past life. Liubov, in *The Cherry Orchard*, reminisces the good old days of the orchard, compensating its present situation and her inadequacy to save it:

> Oh, my childhood, my innocent childhood. I used to sleep in this nursery; I used to look on to the orchard from here, and woke up happy every morning [...] Look, there's Mother walking through the orchard [...] It's no one, I only imagined it.
> (*Orchard*, 347-348)

Characters in Ayckbourn theatre also find realities bitter and hostile, and they do not have the capacity of coping with them. Therefore, they turn away from unpleasant sights and events as it is argued by James C. Coleman that "we refuse to discuss unpleasant topics, [...] we refuse to face our real problems" (87). In Ayckbourn's *Just Between Ourselves*, for example, when confronted with a situation that is disturbing to him, Dennis asserts some contrary belief. Although Vera suffers from "a mental injury," in a state of catatonic schizophrenia, he wants to believe that his wife is "a lot better. She's making giant strides" (*Ourselves*, 63-64). Uncomfortable about Vera's mental death, Dennis is likely "to join in what might be called a denial conspiracy in which any admission of the hopeless condition is avoided" (Martin, 91). Not only do the characters often deny unpleasant reality like Dennis does in *Just Between Ourselves*, they also tend to construct a world in fantasy, as they would like it to be by distorting the reality. The frustration of the characters leads them through disillusionment with the world they live in as the actual world offers them no accomplishment and hence no satisfaction. Any attempt towards fulfillment and happiness is somehow frustrated. This makes the individual feel trapped in an unhappy world, and when the characters of Chekhov and Ayckbourn drama feel miserable with frustrations, the escape for them is their fantasy worlds in which every unattainable wish of the characters is fulfilled. Coleman states: "Fantasy grows essentially out of mental images associated with need gratification. It is stimulated by frustrated desires, for in fantasy the person achieves his goals and gratifies his needs" (87). Both Chekhov's and Ayckbourn's dramatic people try to reach out their ideals in their fantasies since there is no other way of getting a real satisfaction for them.

When Ayckbourn's Susan in *Woman in Mind* fails to define her identity as a wife with her real family, she fantasizes her ideal family in which she can define herself as "the charming, intelligent, spoiled darling of an affectionate" husband, Andy (Londré, 96). Susan compensates for her unhappy husband-wife relationship in her real family by fantasizing a well-adjusted and happy relationship with an imaginary husband; and she finds the self-definition as a wife in this alternate family particularly when her imaginary husband whispers "You're my wife. I love you" (*Mind*, 3). Therefore, Susan fantasizes a self-definition for her role as a wife as well because it is quite clear that the "scenes of fantasy […] vividly portray the kind of self-definition [Susan] would desire" (Londré, 96). Furthermore, as it has already been discussed, Susan lives a sluggish life without an occupation, contributing nothing to the family life but "watch[ing] far too much television […] watch[ing] such trash most of the time" (*Mind*, 22). Unable to face that reality, she begins to reorganize it according to her wishes, and so the failure of establishing "a social identity" is compensated by Susan's fantasy world again. She imagines herself being a famous writer. Her fantasy daughter, Lucy breaks the good news that "last Sunday in the *Observer*, they called you [Susan] probably our most important living historical novelist" (*Mind*, 19). Then, in her hallucinations, Lucy defines Susan as a doctor: "Do you know what is said in the *Sunday Times* about you? It said you were the most brilliant woman heart surgeon there was in this country" (*Mind*, 37). With regard to these quotations above, it can be claimed that Susan makes up a wishful self-definition through her fantasy family, "tak[ing] refuge in a fantasy world where [...] a brilliant daughter idolize her" (Hornby, 110). As this shows, when Susan is frustrated in her real life, she seeks satisfaction in her fantasy world; in other words, her fantasy world is how Susan copes with her frustration. She substitutes her present life with the dream of an ideal to cope with her frustration as the sisters in Chekhov's play "substitute the dream of Moscow for the dream of earthly paradise" (Valency, 187).

Frustration shows its ultimate consequence on people as wasted lives of the characters. Chekhov and Ayckbourn characters see their lives as wasted and unlived. For any of Chekhov's characters, "his life is drawing to a close, and he still has not started to live. Fortune has passed him by; it has not provided him what he sought or what he hoped to achieve" (Paperny, 162); and Ayckbourn's characters, at the play's end, seem bereft, regarding their past lives as wasted. The words, "I realized I'd been doing all the wrong things," echoes in Ayckbourn's plays (*Friends*, 41). Chekhov and Ayckbourn portray characters struggling with dissatisfaction. Their characters are unhappy but they usually do not know the reason for this; they cannot realize that their passive nature is the real cause of their frustrations, and that their discontentment is of their own making. Buried deep into their small worlds, none of the characters can attain happiness. "We're not happy and we can't be happy: we only want happiness," utters Vershinin (*Sisters*, 284).

ALIENATION

Alienation describes the break between human beings in Chekhov's and Ayckbourn's plays. The two playwrights' dramatic characters are alienated figures who live in a state of estrangement with the people around them and with the objective world. Chekhov portrays his characters as lonely, isolated individuals by nature, thus loneliness is argued to be the dominant streak in their character. They are disconnected from the community in which they live and detached from face-to-face relations. That is why Chekhov's theatre reflects people unrelated to anything or to anyone at all in spite of the seemingly close family and/or social relationships. The human condition is essentially one of alienation in Ayckbourn's theatre too, remodeling Chekhov's lonely, isolated individuals in his plays. He dramatizes his characters with the same character trait of loneliness; i.e. the same isolated figures crowd his drama, too. The alienated person in Ayckbourn's plays is similarly unable to relate to his family members, his friends or his fellowmen.

There are seemingly close relations among the people in Chekhov's plays; that is, most of the characters in his drama are relatives and/or engaged in a love triangle. A strong affinity is expected, for example, between Sonia and her father in *Uncle Vanya* or between Arkadina and Konstantin in *The Seagull* as mother and son. However, despite the father-daughter connection between the Professor and Sonia, and mother-son relation between Arkadina and Konstantin, detachment governs their relations because none of Chekhov's characters knows how to relate to the others. There occur only two instances in *Uncle Vanya* where Sonia directs her speech to her father but neither of these dialogues are the attempts for real communication. Therefore, it can be claimed that there is no sharing and/or exchange of feelings, ideas, and responses through the dialogues in Chekhov's plays. In *The Seagull*, similarly, the conversation between Arkadina and Konstantin does not enable them to share any of their feelings, which inevitably leads the son into loneliness.

The relations in Ayckbourn's drama are commonly constructed on marital ties where one expects the most intimate sharing. Almost all his plays dramatize husband-wife relationships but, contrary to usual expectations, his married couples are not so close to each other because, as it is in Chekhov's plays, the characters do not know how to relate to each other. In any marriage of Ayckbourn's plays, there is a lack of understanding and emotional sharing between husbands and wives; and especially the male characters, as has been analyzed, are depicted as the obvious reason for such a lack since they are portrayed as uncomprehending husbands who are oblivious to their wives' emotional needs. Male characters' deafness, however, comes from their inability to figure out ways of getting on well with anybody, the inability which comes to the surface with the playwright's preface to *Just Between Ourselves*. In this preface, Ayckbourn describes Dennis as "a man pathologically incapable of understanding beyond a certain level" (*Ourselves*, 7).

Those who are unable to establish a healthy connection with others in Chekhov's and Ayckbourn's theatre try to avoid the company of their fellowmen by engaging themselves with some solitary occupations such as reading, listening to music or dealing with some hobbies. Both playwrights' characters retreat into their own separate worlds, feeling more secure and comfortable when they do not interact with anybody. This is the self-willed isolation of the characters since it increases the dissociation among them to confine themselves deliberately into seclusion. Isolated Masha in Chekhov's *The Three Sisters* reads a book to prevent the others' company. The stage direction points out, "Masha, in a black dress, is reading a book, her hat on her lap" (*Sisters*, 248); and it is seen that she is so lost in deep thought that she is unaware of what is happening around her. Marina in *Uncle Vanya* is similarly blind to her surrounding in that she spends most of her time in the same solitary occupation, reading. Her eyes never rise from the pages of a pamphlet; "tea is put before her, she drinks it without looking up" (*Vanya*, 193). Thus, she cannot realize the predicament of her son, Vanya, and cannot help him. Vanya suffers alone and his mother's attitude is the cause of dissociation between them.

Reading again is the most convenient retreat among Ayckbourn's characters, too, and it is used to ignore the presence of other people. Evelyn, in *Absent Friends*, disengages herself from the company of the people by reading and so not listening to them. She is regarded as a "strong silent woman" (*Friends*, 45). In *A Small Family Business*, Samantha lives in isolation like Evelyn and like Chekhov's characters. She is a recluse who avoids any interaction with other people by engaging herself with reading. The stage direction makes it known that "she ignores [everybody], apparently engrossed in her book" (*Business*, 12). There are some interruptions from others but she finds ways of aborting these, too: "Samantha is now reading while listening to her personal stereo" (*Business*, 10). She retreats into a world that is impenetrable. However, it is not a blissful world, for it makes her unsocialized:

> Poppy: Oh, Sammy, why don't you go in there and socialize? They'd all love you to socialize. Go on.
> Samantha: (Resuming her book) I don't want to socialize.
> (*Business*, 12)

Sammy's reading a book or locking herself into her room opens a breach between her and her parents. She creates a world of her own in her room and this solitary world is unreachable both literally and figuratively. Her father, Jack says: "It's like Fort Knox trying to get into her room. It's got a combination lock, have you seen it?" (*Business*, 11).

Ayckbourn's male characters shun the company of others, especially of their wives, by creating a world of their own in which they feel totally free from the burden of relating with anyone. In *Just Between Ourselves*, Dennis's garage is such a place where he can escape from the outer world —from dissatisfaction, from Vera and her demands —as Youssef points out in her study, "Dennis runs away from their unhappy marriage into his garage" (14). The reason for this isolation is the fact that he does not know how to associate with his wife. He is unable to understand Vera and he does not know how to show his real feelings of love for his wife, so it is not sometimes his real intention if he does something that upsets Vera. He teases his wife before the guests but this does not directly show he is intentionally cruel or mean since he is not aware of Vera' getting offended with the teasing. Ayckbourn points out in his preface to the play that "Dennis, the husband, is no calculating villain. Nor is he, I contend, particularly unusual. Just a man pathologically incapable of understanding beyond a certain level" (*Ourselves*, 7). For Dennis, the consequence is the failure to relate himself with his wife, and he retreats into isolation embodied with his garage. Dennis, like Samantha, does not want his private world conquered by the outsiders. He lives in his garage and does not let anybody in —especially Vera. The garage door does not yield easily to Vera because it needs mending. Thus, the unfixed garage door is the way that Dennis chooses in order to make his world unconquerable.

Dennis's garage is a heavenly place for him and it becomes a heavenly place for Neil, another male character in the play, too. Like Dennis, Neil flees from his wife by becoming a regular visitor of the garage with the pretext of seeing Dennis's car. Pam complains: "Every other evening, I'm just going to have another look at that car, he says, and off he goes" (*Ourselves*, 36).

In *Woman in Mind*, Gerald's study room is like Dennis's garage in many ways. Gerald is a vicar and he is trying his hand at writing a book about the history of the parish dating back to thirteen eighty-six, but it is clear that his book is just a pretext which he uses to justify his absence. Rather, he tries to avoid the company of his wife by shutting himself up in his study room. Therefore, his study becomes Gerald's solitary world where he lives in isolation from the others. Likewise, Gerald's son, Rick, creates his secluded world in the sect which he joined in order not to be in contact with his family. The sect forbids any verbal contact of its members with their families, so Rick has talked to neither his mother nor his father for two years. Like the other Ayckbournian male characters, Rick draws himself back into his own seclusion and thus "preserves his vow of silence on his increasingly rare visits home" (Billington, 193).

The overall effect of this conscious seclusion especially of male characters is the break between couples, and also painful loneliness on the side of women characters in Ayckbourn's theatre. For Ayckbourn's married women, their husbands' living in seclusion is the sign of bitter negligence, triggering a sense of isolation and loneliness. In *Just Between Ourselves*, it is seen that Vera feels neglected by Dennis, who spends all his time in his garage showing no emotional care for her. While Vera lives all alone at home with her mother-in-law, Dennis busies himself with repairing trivial things. Another Ayckbournian woman character suffering from loneliness due to her husband's deliberate retreat into his isolated world is Susan in *Woman in Mind*. What irritates Susan about Gerald's writing a book is that it takes most of Gerald's time to study in his room and Susan feels neglected emotionally. Making a joke about it, she complains thus: "Gerald's been working on it since thirteen eighty-six [...]. We'd probably have had more [children] if it hadn't been for my husband's book" (*Mind*, 23). Susan sees herself as the ignored and lonely woman in the house; and Gerald "seeks to justify years of sexual and emotional neglect by the fact that he is writing a 60-page history of the parish" (Billington, 183). It is seen in the play that the loss of sharing between Susan and Gerald is at its extreme. Susan points out: "We don't kiss —we hardly touch each other – we don't make love —we don't even share the same bed now. We sleep at different ends of the room" (*Mind*, 13). Moreover, Susan has been separated from her son who withdraws himself to his Therapist order. It can be understood that she tries to fill her loneliness with reminisces of the past, and it is obvious that she tries to console herself with Rick's belongings in his son's absence when she blurts out, "But ... That's all that's left of him ... if we sell his bed [...] I won't be able to sit in there, now. Like I do" (*Mind*, 25). Michael Holt sees these unguarded words of Susan as windows through which "we glimpse a picture of a profoundly lonely woman, sitting in her son's empty room, seeking comfort" (32).

Ayckbourn, in his attempt to project the future of modern man in *Henceforward*, reflects man's submission to mechanical controls as another cause of his characters' detachment in their relations. Technology, which should practically serve man in communication, comes to be his enemy that prevents him from any real close interaction with people. "We have reached a point in history where knowledge and tools intended originally to serve man now threaten to destroy him," observes Eric Josephson in *Man Alone: Alienation in Modern Society* where he discusses the alienation of modern man owing to machines (9). In *Henceforward*, Jerome reaches that point of alienation. He confesses: "I haven't really talked to anyone —well, no face to face —for some time, you see. Since they fully automated the hypermarkets, I don't think I've spoken to anyone for months" (*Henceforward*, 37). The glory belongs to the machines at the end when man regards it as the part of his own body as can be observable in the comic scene below:

> Mervyn: Of course. Now, to the reason we've all met —
> (Something starts to bleep somewhere about his person) [...]
> Would you excuse me? My bleeper. [...] Sorry. Never far away from the office when you've got one of those.
> (He waves his phone)
> Corinna: I thought you said you had two of them?

Mervyn: Ah, yes. I have my private home phone as well. In case my wife wants to get hold of me. [...] Don't worry. I'll put them on to answer. It's the office again, I'll put them on to answer.
(He fumbles in another pocket as he continues to beep)
Jerome: (Intrigued) You have an answering machine on you as well?
Corinna: If you turn him upside down, he also makes ice-cream.
Mervyn: (Rather proudly) I've got a few wires about my person, yes, I have to admit it.

(*Henceforward*, 63-66)

Ayckbourn depicts in *Henceforward* that man is extremely submissive to technology to the point that he becomes reduced to nothingness without it. Jerome's over submission to computers and digital screens makes him an alienated individual communicating with keyboards and screens; i.e. he lives in a "computerised banker surrounded by keyboards, synclaviers and video screens flashing up messages" (Billington, 195). He depersonalizes himself so effectively that he comes to be living with an android as he is unable to relate to his wife and daughter. Unable to establish a healthy relationship with anyone, he makes the android Nan300F his partner. He "relates more easily to [Nan300F] than people," says Billington while discussing Jerome's case (195).

Indifferent Individuals

One reason that helps to widen the break between individuals is the indifferent streak in the characters' nature in Chekhov's and Ayckbourn's plays. Both playwrights dramatize their characters with certain aloofness to each other owing to their traits of ineptness and selfishness. They are portrayed as self-centered individuals who are constantly indulged in their own concerns and tend to exploit one another by their egoism. The characters' lack of energy and over-interest in their selfish matters create "indifferent parents" who are unsympathetic to their children's cry for emotional care. The parents in Chekhov's and Ayckbourn's dramas do not have the necessary responsibility of being fathers and mothers; therefore, it is most likely to find children in their plays suffering from lack of interest and alienation. Chekhov reflects the inertia of the characters as the primary reason that creates indifferent parents in his plays. Especially female characters in a Chekhov play can be unqualified as mothers since they do not seem to have the necessary capability of bringing up a child because of their lack of energy and interest. Therefore, Chekhov's mother figures very often neglect their offspring. In *The Seagull*, for example, Chekhov portrays Masha as the uncaring mother who does not give proper attention to her duty as a mother by not taking the slightest care of her baby. When her husband, Madviedenko, urges Masha to return to their home for "the baby maybe hungry," she responds indifferently: "What nonsense! Matriona will feed him" (*Sisters*, 166). Masha's negligence and lack of motherly concern become clearer when Madviedenko expresses his worries about the baby: "I feel sorry for him [the baby]. This is the third night he has been without his mother" (*Sisters*, 166). In his criticism of the play, David Magarshack sees Masha's lack of interest and lethargy as the source of her indifference to her own baby. He writes: "She does not care for her child because it requires too much attention and effort" (203).

In Ayckbourn drama, too, the inept and lazy characters make unwilling, inefficient and irresponsible mothers and fathers. These parents do not care for their children's needs for affection and do not pay enough attention to their upbringing. Therefore, they become reluctant parents to look after their offspring. The mother and father figures in Ayckbourn's plays always get rid of the responsibility of parenthood by ignoring their children's basic needs as can be exemplified in *Absent Friends* and *Season's Greetings*. In *Absent Friends*, Evelyn is reminiscent of Chekhov's Masha as the indifferent mother who openly neglects her baby. Diana hints at Evelyn's inadequacy as a mother at the beginning of the play. It is clear that Evelyn lacks the experience of covering up a baby. As a matter of fact, she does not know much about a baby's needs in general:

>Diana: (Anxiously) Should he be covered up as much as that, dear?
>Evelyn: Yes.
>Diana: Won't he get too hot?
>Evelyn: He likes it hot.
>Diana: Oh. I was just worried he wasn't getting enough air.
>Evelyn: He's all right. He doesn't need much air.
>Diana: Oh, well ... (She looks about her)
>
>(*Friends*, 1)

Diana is apprehensive about Evelyn's ability to care for her baby properly. What is more shocking is the scene where the baby is left outside in the rain: "Evelyn: Oh. I'm going to fetch Wayne in. It's raining" (*Friends*, 44). In this scene, Evelyn's indifference and inadequacy as a mother reach its climax in the play. Both Evelyn and Masha are unsympathetic towards their babies because of their laziness; both mothers are negligent, one leaves the baby outside in the rain, the other has not seen her baby for three days; both Evelyn and Masha abandon the duties of motherhood to someone else. Masha expects a servant to feed the baby. Evelyn, likewise, does not show the proper motherly care to baby Wayne; as a result, her husband is responsible for child caring: "He's wonderful with that baby. [...] Does all the things a mother should and better" (*Friends*, 33).

In *Season's Greetings*, Ayckbourn depicts a male character this time as the indifferent parent who neglects the charges of a father. Eddie's negligence as a father is conveyed throughout the whole play. Pattie, his wife, calls Eddie upstairs to help put one of their children into bed. However, Eddie ignores this call many a time inventing some excuses. During the whole act Pattie keeps calling Eddie upstairs and the latter endlessly ignores that duty. Finally, he yields reluctantly after many calls from his wife:

>Pattie: (grimly) You coming or not?
>(Eddie wearily puts down his glass and starts up the stairs quite slowly. Pattie waits for him on the landing)

> He won't go to sleep till he sees you. He's convinced himself
> now that you're dead.
>
> (*Greetings*, 13)

The emphasis lies on the point that the boy sees his father so rarely that he believes his father is dead. This seems to be a part of Ayckbourn's comedy, a very trivial point to rely on. Nonetheless, there are some other scenes which support the fact that Eddie is an uncaring father to his children. As a father, he does not spend much time with them. When Pattie wants him to go for a walk together with the children, Eddie refuses to go, although he has promised before. It is clear that he cannot bear the existence of his children because he feels it requires too much attention and effort, for example, to go for a walk with the kids (*Greetings*, 24). Thus, the lack of energy and selfishness makes Eddie an indifferent father as it makes Masha an indifferent mother in *The Seagull*; and being an indifferent father, Eddie leaves his wife on her own with all the responsibilities of looking after the children although she is seven-month pregnant.

The selfish nature of the characters is another reason for indifferent parents in Chekhov's and Ayckbourn's plays. Parents who are always engrossed in their own matters become oblivious to their children's needs and concerns. Among Chekhov's plays, this is quite pronounced in *The Seagull* and *Uncle Vanya*. In *The Seagull*, Arkadina is heedless of her son's genius. Her son, Konstantin, composes plays for the stage, but she never treasures or comments on any of them. This is not because Konstantin is an untalented writer; many in the acting profession find him talented (*Seagull*, 176), but this is because Arkadina lacks interest in her son's works. She is completely absorbed in her so-called talent as an actress and in the life she is living far away from her son. Her lack of interest in and understanding of Konstantin's talent is most manifest when she confesses: "Can you imagine? —I haven't read anything of his yet. There's never any time" (*Seagull*, 176). She has never spared time for her son and his genius. David Magarshack sees Arkadina as the chief destroyer of Konstantin's talent with her remoteness. He contends: "Arkadina tramples on and utterly destroys the spark of genius in her son because she is quite incapable of appreciating it" (192). *Uncle Vanya*, on the other hand, renders Professor Serebriokov as another Chekhovian example of an indifferent parent. He is aloof from her daughter because of his own interests in his selfish concerns. He spends his whole life in Moscow far away from his daughter for the sake of his seemingly academic carrier, which means he does not give enough care to Sonia.

Like Chekhov's Arkadina and the Professor, Jerome in Ayckbourn's *Henceforward* is reflected as the indifferent father due to his over emphasis on his own interests. Jerome is so selfishly stuck in his own job that he completely neglects his daughter and his wife, living separated from them. He does not even recognize his daughter who has turned into "a shorthaired, dark-chinned hermaphrodite" teenager (*Henceforward*, 74). In *A Small Family Business,* Jack as a father ignores his daughter's problems in the same way. When the private detective informs him about his daughter's shoplifting, Jack never tries to inquire about the reasons why his daughter, Samantha, did such a thing. He never wants to understand her, and finally to help her. Being a symbol of "morality" in the play, he is interested only in the "immorality" of Samantha's action and blames her for the disgrace she brings on his name. Since morality is everything for Jack, it is not important for him whether Samantha will be imprisoned or not. When the private detective offers him a way out that will save Samantha, Jack simply refuses to settle a bargain with the detective because of his selfish idealism of morality, hence he "allows his daughter to be prosecuted" (Billington, 190). When the other family members react against his selfishness, Jack's response underlines once again his indifference to his own daughter: "Look, to hell with Sammy" (*Business*, 32).

Chekhov argues in his plays that the parenthood is a burden for his inert and egocentric characters. Between the lines, he gives the hints that the parents in his plays are unwilling to take over the charge of parenthood. Ayckbourn develops this character trait in his drama. He analyzes the parent-child relationship nearly in every one of his plays. Like Chekhov, he reflects mothers and fathers for whom parenthood is nothing but a burden; therefore, they try to escape from the responsibility of child upbringing. As a result, in both dramatists' works the indifference of parents to their children causes a lack of communication and alienation between both sides, and suffering offspring. In Chekhov's *The Seagull*, the gap between Arkadina and Konstantin is so wide that there is no healthy communication between the mother and the son. Both of them are unable to express their true feelings towards one another, so their conversation is sometimes tenderly, and sometimes very aggressive as if it were between two strangers (*Seagull*, 158-159).

In Ayckbourn's *Woman in Mind*, there is an obvious loss of communication between Susan and her son. Susan's selfish concerns hinder any kind of conversation between the two. Rick's playing the deaf and mute with his parents is the symbolic embodiment of loss of communication between the parents and their children in Ayckbourn drama. To highlight the loss of communication between two generations, Ayckbourn uses another son, Christopher, in *Joking Apart*, who never talks to either of his parents, Louise and Hugh. In any Ayckbourn play, parents who have grown up children suffer from an inability to communicate with them. In *Joking Apart*, the aloofness between Christopher and his parents is the result of the former's playing the deaf and mute with them:

> Anthea: Louise has been —you know, peculiar again. [...] Don't whatever you do ask her after Christopher.
> Olive: Something wrong?
> Anthea: With Christopher? No, he's fine. [...] Only he won't speak to them, that's the trouble. He really is a weird youth when you meet him. You can almost hear this brain going round as he stares at you. Quite spooky. He's completely cut off from Louise and Hugh. He's quite gentle with them. He treats them like a couple of deaf-mute family retainers.
> Olive: Oh dear.
> Anthea: It's one of the reasons for Louise's condition, of course. She has her high days and low days, a bit like the church. It de-

pends what miracle drug the doctor's currently got her on. She can be anything from soporific to suicidal.

(*Apart*, 186-187)

The indifferent parents prove to be failures as mothers and fathers. They fail to bring up affectionate and mentally healthy children who are at laze with their parents. Both Chekhov and Ayckbourn depict suffering children who are brought up by inadequate, irresponsible and indifferent parents. Such children fail to develop a healthy and balanced identity when they grow up. Samantha is the suffering offspring of Ayckbourn's *A Small Family Business*. Jack's negligence of his daughter widens the gap between the father and the daughter. He hardly speaks to Samantha, and similarly she is shy to express her feelings to her father, and as a result of Jack's indifference to her, she is driven to drug addiction. Michael Billington accuses Jack as the only one responsible for Samantha's taking drugs: "[Jack] is a negligent father whose indifference to Samantha has pushed her into the reclusive world of drugs" (190).

Ayckbourn makes it clearer in *Joking Apart* why Christopher is suffering now as a grown up young boy since in this play he supplies his audience with the necessary information concerning Christopher's upbringing from his babyhood to teenage years. This also directly represents the failure of Christopher's parents, Hugh and Louise, in child upbringing. When the play opens Christopher is only four and a half years old; and just in the beginning of the play he proves to be a "naughty boy". While two families are in the garden enjoying themselves with fireworks, Christopher, to everyone else's surprise, does "a wee-wee in the fireworks" (*Apart*, 139). For a four-and-half-year-old kid it is quite normal to urinate on something that makes him "a bit over excited" and cry (*Apart*, 137). On the other hand, the reaction of Hugh and Louise to that action of their boy's is not normal. They shout at him and finally Louise takes him home as a punishment:

Hugh: Christopher. Christopher, you naughty boy. Stop that.

> Louise: (simultaneously) Christopher, Christopher, you little beast. Hugh, stop him.
> Richard: (simultaneously) Oy, oy, oy.
> Hugh: You naughty boy. You naughty boy, naughty boy.
> Hugh goes into the court and disappears.
> Louise: (following him) Right, Christopher, I'm taking you straight home. I'm taking you straight home this minute. I'm taking him straight home, Hugh.
>
> (Apart, 139)

Having no understanding why Christopher does such a thing, Hugh and Louise expect a grown up man's behavior from the child: a grown up man does not urinate on fireworks when it threatens him. The failure of the parents here is that they do not question and try to figure out the reason behind Christopher's action.

During the later years, Christopher becomes more and more "naughty," angry and stubborn, and we learn that someone else takes care of him instead of his mother. When they go somewhere or have something to do, the grandmother or a nurse usually looks after Christopher. This, of course, prevents the little kid from the necessary affection of his own mother and father; in turn, the lack of motherly affection makes him more stubborn, a nuisance and sometimes an enemy against his parents. Christopher is getting impossible and the parents do not know how to deal with that growing boy:

> Louise: He's just been absolutely impossible. The little brute, he just screamed and yelled. I had to leave him to Hugh. He's getting too strong for me now. He's eight years old and when he punches you, it really hurts.
>
> (Apart, 155)

The lack of communication between Christopher and his parents becomes serious. In the final act of the play, he is now a young man. Still the others see him as an abnormal individual, "secretive, very contained" (*Apart*, 178). He does not talk with his mother and father, which illustrates the serious gap between the child and the parents initiated by the lack of interest and affection in his upbringing. The parents are not aware that Christopher suffers as an asocial human being.

The selfish nature of the characters both in Chekhov's and Ayckbourn's plays is the very cause of indifferent individuals and especially indifferent parents. This reflects the characters in both playwrights' drama as unqualified mothers and fathers. Christine Youssef, criticizing the failure of mothers in an Ayckbourn play, argues in her work that "not all couples automatically make good parents, and not all women automatically make good mothers in an Ayckbourn play" (39). The indifference between children and parents causes in turn their alienation from each other and loneliness on both sides.

Inadequate Language and Non-Communication

It comes to be a common trend in the Western theatre, particularly with the appearance of the Absurdist tradition, to draw attention to "the lack of communication" of modern man. With his plays reflecting the alienation that modern man experiences, Alan Ayckbourn has changed the focus of the issue to the "difficulty of communication," or rather the impossibility of it (Kirca, 129). Martin Esslin's observations for Pinter's use of language to argue that language constructs an obstacle for communication in Absurd Drama can also describe how Ayckbourn pursues the same issue in his plays. He contends:

> Instead of any inability to communicate, there is a deliberate evasion of communication. Communication itself between people is so frightening that rather than do that there is continual crosstalk, a continual talking about other things, rather than what is at the root of their relationship.
>
> (Esslin, 244)

It is widely accepted that "nothing is as potent as language in bridging our separateness from one another," for language is believed to enable us "to share our most intimate thoughts" (Weston, 277). It is supposed to be "the function of signs to reflect inward experiences or objects in the real world to make present one's thoughts and feelings" (Eagleton, 129). In Ayckbourn's drama, however, language is not the medium that bridges the gap between the characters. Instead, it is reflected as an inadequate system to produce immediate meaning, and therefore, to transfer his characters' thoughts and feelings. On the contrary, language is seen as an obstacle itself in the way of communication in his plays.

The representation of language in both Chekhov's and Ayckbourn's plays can be said to prefigure post-structuralist theories on language. Post-structuralist theory views language as an imprecise, and therefore, as an inadequate device which cannot produce immediate meaning with words because there is, as the theory points out, absence of harmonious "one-to-one set of correspondences between the level of the signifiers and the level of the signifieds in language" (Eagleton, 110-111). It was Saussure's proposition that the combination between the signifier (the sound image or the written form) and the signified (the concept or meaning) is firmly bounded together as the two sides of a single sheet of paper. However, post-structuralist thought argues that, unlike Saussure's claim, the signifier and the signified are not always inseparable and that there is no secure bond between them. In other words, meaning is not a concept attached closely to a particular signifier, but "it is the spin-off of a potentially endless play of signifiers" (Eagleton, 110). The post-structuralist Lacan questions this unity and divides the signifier from the signified; thus, he "opens up a hidden gap between signifier and signified" (Wright, 109). The final implication post-structuralist theory reaches is that language is much less stable and meaning is evasive. A signifier may have more than one signifieds, and similarly, there may be multiple signifiers referring to the same signified. If this is the case that language is unstable and inadequate to reflect inner experiences, thoughts and feelings, Terry Eagleton argues, then "we can never mean precisely what we say and never say precisely what we mean" (169). Since "there is a perpetual sliding of the signified under the signifier," as Lacan states (qtd. in Lodge, 79), meaning comes to be an illusion. Eagleton in his study epitomizes the idea in the following quotation:

> if you want to know the meaning (or signified) of a signifier, you can look it up in the dictionary; but all you will find will be yet more signifiers, whose signifieds you can in turn look up and so on.
>
> (111)

Language reflected in Chekhov's and Ayckbourn's drama is this kind of language that does not permit their characters to communicate what they think and feel. It does serve not as a bridge between man's mind and tongue, or between one character and another. Therefore, it does not yield an understanding and sharing between the individuals, and both playwrights' characters lack genuine communication. Even a slight understanding between them becomes impossible. Hence, the gap between parents and children, between two relatives or friends, in fact, between any two people, gets wider owing to non-communication in the plays of both dramatists.

Chekhov's *Uncle Vanya* introduces the relation between Sonia and Professor Serebriakov as the example for the loss of interaction between the father and the daughter because of the above mentioned impossibility of communication. The lack of communication between them is highlighted by the absence of conversation between the two. There are, as indicated before, only two instances throughout the whole play where Sonia directs her speech to her father (*Vanya*, 203, 231). Nevertheless, neither of these dialogues between them are the attempts for a real communication. The lack of communication between the other characters of the play, too, is conveyed through the non-existence of conversation in *Uncle Vanya*. This especially emerges in the final act of the play where people only say "good bye" to each other at the departure of the Professor and his wife, and Dr. Astrov. As soon as they depart, the remaining characters immediately turn to their own business without uttering any word that would pursue a sharing of feelings. Marina "sits down in an easy chair and knits a stocking," Maryia "becomes absorbed in reading," and Sonia and Vanya "both write in silence" (*Vanya*, 242). Laurence Senelick gives this final scene where conversation is non-existent as an example for the loss of communication in the play:

> The absence of conversation is noticeable in this symbiosis. Were it not for Vanya's impassioned outburst and Sonia's attempts to console him, the characters would write, knit, yawn, read and strum the guitar voicelessly with no need to communicate aloud.
>
> (94)

The inadequacy of language as a medium of communication shows itself in Ayckbourn's drama when the characters "slide from one signifier to another" as they are unable to arrive at a final meaning that they want to communicate. Ayckbourn's characters are unable to find exact, meaningful and appropriate words to transmit their thoughts and emotions but come up only with signifiers. In *Absent Friends*, no one knows how to express his/her grief for Colin's late fiancée. The characters of the play cannot figure out what words to use to convey their feelings and the result is the absence of communication and relation between Colin and his friends. Diana stands up to communicate on behalf of everyone but her attempt to share Colin's grief is just an utter failure:

> Diana: Yes. (Pause) I think I can speak for all of us —(she rises, then sits) —Colin, when I say how very sorry we were to hear about your loss. As I hope you'll realize, we're your friends and – well —and although we didn't know Carol —none of us had the pleasure of meeting her —we feel that in small way, your grief is our grief. After all, in this world, we are all to some extent — we're all —what's the word ...?

> Paul: Joined.
> Diana: No.
> John: Related.
> Marge: Combined.
> Diana: No. Dependent.
> Paul: That's what I said.
> Diana: No you didn't, you said joined or something.
> Paul: It's the same thing. Joined, dependent, means the same.
> Diana: We are all dependent in a way for our own- and, well- no, I'm sorry I've forgotten what I was going to say now. I hope you understand what I meant, anyway.
>
> (*Friends*, 26)

Similar to the poststructuralist view that sees meaning elusive due to the above mentioned "sliding of the signified under the signifier," in this example from *Absent Friends*, characters run from one signifier to another, never reaching the meaning they want to communicate. "Joined, dependent means the same" for Paul, all signifiers, yet they cannot say what they mean. Since meaning is always slippery, Ayckbourn's characters cannot mean what they say, either. This is what happens to Dennis and Vera in *Just Between Ourselves*. They misunderstand each other most of the time. Vera refers to her needs indirectly without being clear what she means by "help":

> Vera: ... I need help, Dennis.
> Dennis: Yes, but don't you see, you're not being clear, Vee. You say help but what sort of help do you mean?
> Vera: Just help. From you.
> Dennis: Yes. Well, look, tell you what. When you've got a moment, why don't you sit down, get a bit of paper and just make a little list of all the things you'd like me to help you with. Things you'd like me to do, things that need mending or fixing and then we can talk about them and see what I can do to help.
>
> (*Ourselves*, 54)

When the characters are unable to express themselves, they have only clichés to talk with. In *A Small Family Business*, anytime Jack and Samantha endeavor to talk, they fail, and they can only achieve some sort of a conversation with clichés. This is another indication of the bankruptcy of language as a medium for communication. Jack is aware of the loss of communication between himself and his daughter, but he does not know the reason for this and he cannot figure out a way to cope with it, complaining "she never listens to me [...]. She hardly talks to me these days at all. Hardly get five words out of her" (*Business*, 28):

> Jack: Hallo, Sammy.
> Samantha: Hallo, dad.
> Jack: Didn't you see there. All right, then?
> Samantha: Yes, I'm all right.
> Jack: Right. (They appear to have run out of conversation) Good.
>
> (*Business*, 10)

Both in Chekhov's and Ayckbourn's plays, there are pauses and dots in abundance to indicate instances when nobody knows what to say and how to communicate with the others. "Dots do the talking" instead of the characters, Ayckbourn points out in an interview (Fay, *Independent*, 4). The pauses where characters find themselves in silence are the great revelations of their emotions. Pauses and dots become more explanatory than their words since words are meaningless, signifying nothing: "Silence, the mouthpiece of destiny, talks as eloquently as words speak meaninglessly" (Barricelli, xiii). For example, in Act II in *The Cherry Orchard*, finally all the characters fall in silence after a futile effort to communicate with each other. This time "all sit absorbed in their thoughts" without any desire for communication, and "there is only the silence," as the stage direction states (*Orchard*, 364). As a result, characters' trust in language and communication is destroyed when they see that language is useless, and that it does not lead them to understanding and sharing. Ayckbourn's characters try to avoid communication and they are much happier without language: "Absolute peace. Neither of us ever says a word to each other. That is the secret of a successful union" (*Friends*, 45). Desmond, in *A Small*

Family Business, "who refuses to talk, refuses to communicate at all," shuts himself in the kitchen to prevent any contact with his wife, Harriet (*Business*, 60). In *Woman in Mind*, Susan's inability to explain herself is the result of inadequacy of language. Her attempts to express herself to Gerald have been a failure since her husband never believes that they can solve the problems in their marriage simply by talking over them:

> Susan: You don't feel we should perhaps talk.
> Gerald: No, I don't quite honestly. I don't at all. I think talking has got us precisely nowhere.
>
> (*Mind*, 38)

Language is reflected by Chekhov and Ayckbourn as an obstacle on the way to communication. After their desperate attempts to conversation, all they can produce is a distortion of what they really mean. They realize language is an insufficient device to present their thoughts and emotions. Therefore, they usually prefer silence to communication.

Disconnected Dialogue

Dialogues in Chekhov's theatre turn into monologues when his characters do not listen to each other attentively or do not respond to one another sensibly. Such a style of "disconnected dialogue" (Magarshack, 169) in his plays creates the image of a character speaking to him/herself, not communicating with the others around; and the playwright uses this primarily "to express the isolation of people from one another" (Bently, 180), that is, to express the alienation of his characters when each one speaks for him/herself and there is no one to listen to. The indifference and alienation of Chekhov's characters are given as the chief reason for their solitary dialogues by Charles W. Meister: "People fail to respond meaningfully to each other's discourse, being lost in absorption with their own concerns" (ix). Therefore, Chekhov's characters attempt to communicate their ideas only in their characteristic dissociated monologues. None of them pays the necessary attention nor replies to the other's discourse, as his/her mind is on something else. This creates a loss of communication among the characters of the play.

In *The Three Sisters*, Andrey reveals his most hidden emotions to Ferapont. Yet, the conversation between the two does not lead to any point because Ferapont's responds to Andrey are out of context and meaningless. Andrey talks about his loneliness whereas Ferapont talks about something absolutely irrelevant. His are "sudden replies that do not seem to be immediately motivated by the context" (Nilsson, 255). This can be observed in the following quotation from the play:

> Andrey: [...] I don't drink and I don't like going to pubs, but my word! How I'd enjoy an hour or so at Tyestov's, or the Great Moscow Restaurant! Yes, my dear fellow, I would indeed!
> Ferapont: The other day at the office a contractor was telling me about some businessmen who were eating pancakes in Moscow. One of them ate forty pancakes and died. It was either forty or fifty, I can't remember exactly.
> Andrey: You can sit in some huge restaurant in Moscow without knowing anyone, and no one knowing you [...]
> Ferapont: What's that? (A pause) It was the same man that told me —of course, he may have been lying —he said that there's an enormous rope stretched right across Moscow.
> (*Sisters*, 275)

The most compact example of Chekhovian "disconnected dialogue" appears in *The Cherry Orchard* in Act II when the characters deliver characteristic monologues of their own without any interaction. Charlotta opens the act with her complaints about her lack of identity, Liubov confesses her sinful past and Lopakhin expresses his practical solutions for the lethargy in Russia while Gayev addresses the sunset. On top of it, Trofimov utters a long speech on Russian society. Thus, all mouth their deeply buried emotions, yet without listening to each other. For instance, none of them listens to Charlotta mindfully. Yepihedov "plays the guitar and sings," and Dooniasha "looks at herself in a hand mirror and powders her face," as the stage directions indicate (*Orchard*, 354-355). Consequently, Charlotta's concerns do not attract anyone's attention, nor do they bring out a response from the others; on the contrary, it is as if she utters a soliloquy.

These two examples from *The Three Sisters* and *The Cherry Orchard* illustrate that in a Chekhov play the characters' flashes of self-revelation can easily be transformed into "static, isolated and disconnected statements of opinion" (Magarshack, 169). The disconnected dialogue of Chekhov's plays is the outcome of the characters' lack of interest in others' concerns and their over indulgence in selfish pursuits. When one person utters his/her ideas, emotions or problems, the other one, immersed in personal concerns, is reminded of something totally irrelevant. The consequence is a prevalent absence of communication and alienation among Chekhov's characters. Although the characters are in a desperate need to communicate to the others, they fail to do so, and end up being very lonely.

In Ayckbourn's drama, Chekhovian "disconnected dialogue" becomes more pronounced and ridiculous when the characters ruin any hope of communication by either not listening or not responding to their correspondents or by cross talking. Ayckbourn's characters, too, pay little attention to what is said to them, and go off in a tangent in their replies. His characters have no sense of timing, either. They choose the worst possible moment to bring out their problems. In *A Small Family Business*, while Harriet is talking with Poppy about her serious problems, the latter is totally engrossed in preparing the table for a dinner party and does not respond to Harriet. Instead, she is busy giving directions to someone else, which creates the comic scene below:

> Harriet: I cannot face going into our kitchen these days. I get as far as the door and I cannot even bring myself to go in there to soak a bag of tea.
> Poppy: (At the hatch, to Tina) No, the other side, love. That's it. (Tina replies once more).

> Harriet: I can hear him in there grilling and stewing till all hours of the night. I can smell it for the rest of the day. [...] (Tearfully) He's in there all weekend making these huge meals. Three or four courses at a time ... (Shudders).
> Poppy: Look, I promise you, Harriet, you can come round whenever you like. Any evening. I'll be only too happy to listen, dear. But not just at the moment, my love.
>
> (*Business*, 15)

Similarly, in *Absent Friends*, when Diana pours out her problems to Marge that her husband has an affair with Evelyn, a lady friend of them, Marge does not seem to be giving an ear to her complaints. Her whole concentration is on the things that she has bought, so instead of answering Diana, she wonders which pair of shoes would suit her dress. As a result, there is no interaction between even the so-called friends. Whatever is up most in their minds, they seem to have an urge to bring that out:

> Diana: I know she [Evelyn]'s been up to something. I don't trust her. [...] She and Paul. I know they have.
> Marge: Well ... (Producing a pair of very unsuitable shoes). There, you see. Aren't they nice?
>
> (*Friends*, 5)

Ayckbourn's characters seem as if they do not actually hear what is being said to them. Billington points to the fact that this inability to hear is presented symbolically with the actual noise that screens out hearing in *Just Between Ourselves*. Neil tries to symptomize what is wrong in his marriage and wants to discuss it with Dennis but the whole conversation is inaudible because of Dennis's drilling. The whole dialogue does not make sense due to "the inability, even refusal, of one character to listen to another" (Peace, 128), which is physically presented with the drone of the drill:

> Neil: ... you see, my trouble —Pam's trouble is this. I think we —
> (Dennis starts drilling, the rest is inaudible)

—both expect things from each other. Things that the other one is not prepared to give —
(Dennis stops drilling)
—to the other one. Do you get me? [...] You have your opposites —like this
(He holds up his hands to demonstrate)
(Dennis starts drilling)
This is me —that's her. And they attract —
(Dennis stops drilling)
—like a magnet.
(Dennis starts again)
Only with people opposed to magnets, the trouble is with people —[...]
(He looks to Dennis for a reaction to this)
(Dennis drills. Neil waits. Dennis stops).

(*Ourselves*, 47)

Chekhovian disconnected dialogue in *Season's Greetings* is the device to deduce the lack of communication between husband and wife, Neville and Belinda. When Belinda attempts to express her feelings about their relationship and to comment on their marriage, Neville only seems to be listening to her but actually he does not pay the slightest attention to his wife. During their conversation, he is totally engrossed into fiddling some toy and "mm" is his chief response to Belinda (*Greetings*, 36).

It is obvious that the disconnected dialogue in both playwrights' theatre is a way of showing life's isolation; the alienated characters can only produce unrelated conversations. However, its effect on the characters is harmful in that it makes them suffer because they get no feedback to help them with their problems and they end up leading insular lives due to lack of communication. "I must talk to someone, but my wife doesn't seem to understand me, and as for my sisters ... I'm afraid of them for some reason or other. I'm afraid of them laughing at me and pulling my leg," echoes Andrey's voice in all Chekhov's plays (*Sisters*, 274-275), and Ayckbourn's as well.

Self-Estrangement

Alienation in Chekhov's and Ayckbourn's drama does not denote only the break between individuals but it also signifies dissociation from self due to detachment from others and from the world at large. It is argued that "one acquires a self or identity by communicating with others, especially through language" (Josephson, 15); nonetheless, as is understood from the above examples, both playwrights' characters become detached in close relations and from the community in which they live. Therefore, estrangement among both playwrights' characters results in their alienation from their selves, i.e. they lose their identity or selfhood through isolation. Even though it is known that man acquires a self through interaction with people, the inadequacy of language chokes the means of communication not only with others but also with one's self as well. There is the strong necessity for language "when man looks into his mind or searches his soul" (Eagleton, 112); but according to post-structuralist theory, the meaning of signs is absent —signs with which, as Terry Eagleton points out, one searches his soul and tries to reflect it; thus, man can never reach "any full communion with himself" (112). Discussing the post-structuralist theory of self, Eagleton makes it clear that "not only my meaning but me" cannot be fully present "since language is something I am made out of" (112). Post-structuralist thought necessitates that in conscious life we achieve a sense of ourselves as unified beings but this image of ourselves as unified beings is an imaginary one just like the imaginary situation that occurs when a person contemplates himself in the mirror and has the illusion that his appearance reflected back to him can represent the wholeness of his being. Thus,

> the imagery representation of ourselves, the mirror image, is incapable of providing us with a stable identity ... [and] the only option left for acquiring [identity] seems to be the field of linguistic representation, the symbolic register, seeking in language a means to acquire a stable identity.
> (Stavrakakis, 18-20)

The individual hopes to gain an adequate representation through language but this is a futile effort. In the mirror image, man is the signifier and the image in the mirror the signified; and "there is not any real unity between the self (signifier) and its meaning, identity" (Eagleton, 146). Likewise, in the symbolic stage there is, as it is in language, a gap between the signifier and its identity (signified). Therefore, self is not a unified, stable identity according to Lacanian thought; in other words, "we are never able to recover the pure self-identity" (Eagleton, (146).

In the light of the arguments referred to, it is safe to claim that isolation and non-communication in Chekhov's and Ayckbourn's drama result in their characters' alienation from their selves as well as from each other. The characters who recoil from getting in touch with other people are unable to get in touch with themselves. These lead the characters to a state of selflessness. They gradually get deprived of some part of themselves and come to be detached from their own feelings. They are now even strangers to themselves and to their emotions, so they cannot define and formulate their emotions. Consequently, they suffer from an inability to express their innermost feelings and thoughts to the other people around. The characters of Chekhov's drama try to evade self-expression that will reveal their hidden ideas and emotions, so the language becomes evasive and inadequate while a character tries to put into words his innermost feelings. Likewise, Ayckbourn's characters do not feel at ease when they are to reveal their buried emotions. The failure of self-expression in Ayckbourn's drama is the most overt manifestation for characters' alienation from their selves.

Loss of self-expression of Chekhov's characters serves as the main cause of his characters' self-alienation. In *The Three Sisters*, Andrey tries to avoid putting his thoughts into words. He verbalizes his emotions to Ferapont only, for Andrey knows that Ferapont is half-deaf and unable to understand him. Otherwise, Andrey would never make the confession of his genuine, innermost feelings to him:

Andrey: [...] Good Heavens! Just think —I'm secretary of the local council now, and Protopopov's chairman, and the most I can ever hope for is to become a member of the council myself! [...] I, who dream every night that I'm a professor in Moscow University, a famous academician, the pride of all Russia!
Ferapont: I'm sorry, I can't tell you. I don't hear very well.
Andrey: If you could hear properly I don't think I'd be talking to you like this.

(Sisters, 274)

Gayev's billiard terms in *The Cherry Orchard* show his inadequacy to communicate his thoughts or feelings through words. He constantly uses terms in his talk like "red one into the corner pocket" and "I cut into the side pocket" and so on; and he usually utters them when he is expected to define his emotions. He completes his sentences with these billiard terms since he does not know what to say about himself. Nils Ake Nilsson sheds light on the functions of Gayev's using these terms thus: "The terms serve, in other words, as a cover for feelings he is unable to express, as system of signals that appeals to the intuition of the listeners" (255).

Characters' failure to articulate their emotions comes to the surface as one of the evidences for self-estrangement in Ayckbourn's drama as well. His characters, too, need a camouflage to hide their emotions when they are to pronounce them. In *Just Between Ourselves*, the function of Dennis's laughter is identical with Gayev's billiard terms. It is a way to cover up his feelings and to escape from uttering them. Everything is "just between ourselves" for Dennis, not for people at large, as Billington points out, and there is a "fear of expressing emotions" in Dennis (111). Whenever he is expected to reveal his self, emotions and thoughts, there comes Dennis's noisy laughter, "a laugh that keeps all emotion, fear, panic and sensitivity at bay" (Billington, 111).

Alienation and estrangement of the characters comes to be an insoluble problem in Ayckbourn's plays because of female failure to express themselves. The dramatist's women characters are regarded as "suffering from aphasia" —total or partial loss of the ability to use or understand language —owing to the failure of self-expression (Kalson, 107). Ayckbourn's married women are unable to explain themselves thoroughly to their husbands; they have wishes and needs but they fail to phrase their expectations and the reasons for them. Ayckbourn indicates in his preface to *Just Between Ourselves* that Vera is "hampered by a lack of ability to express herself clearly" (*Ourselves*, 7). She cannot put forward openly what she needs and what she means by "help"; she refers to this indirectly only. As a result, her cries for emotional "help" is answered by Dennis's "mending and fixing" since she does not clearly sort it out what she means by help.

The post-structuralists treat self as not a stable entity. In this sense, Chekhov's and Ayckbourn's characters turn into non-entities suffering from a certain lack of self-identity. They no longer feel certain who they are because they are alienated from their fellowmen and alienated from themselves. Both playwrights' characters are unable to acquire a stable identity for themselves and begin to question their existing identities. In Chekhov's *The Cherry Orchard*, Charlotta is the one who cannot figure out a self-definition for herself; she complains from lack of identity: "When Papa and Mama died, a German lady took me into her house and began to give me lessons. So then I grew up and became a governess. But where I come from and who I am, I don't know" (*Orchard*, 354). In Ayckbourn's drama, the lack of communication and isolation between the characters bring the female figures to the brink of self-alienation since his women characters are incapable of defining their roles and of constructing an identity for themselves, as it has already been exemplified in *Just Between Ourselves* and *Woman in Mind* in the previous part. When Ayckbourn's women characters are unable to define their roles either as housewives, mothers or working people, it has been claimed that they gradually lose their identities as wives, mothers and as career women, and like Charlotta in *The Cherry Orchard*, Ayckbourn's women characters begin to question their selves. Isolation between the characters causes their being estranged to their own feelings and thoughts, and personalities. They become dehumanized and deprived of the definite, stable shell called "identity".

VICIOUS CIRCLE

Chekhov's and Ayckbourn's passive, unfulfilled, and isolated individuals experience a sort of entrapment when they become hopeless and aimless people who are unable to change any single aspect of their lives. They are trapped in a vicious circle of dull routine and utter boredom, and they do not find in themselves the necessary life energy to change the cyclic quality of their lives. Chekhov's characters, at the beginning of his plays, are generally born into the utter boredom of provincial life. They find country life as the source of their ineptitude, unproductivity and dullness; it is the center of "stagnant existence" (*Seagull*, 155). They are caught "in this crypt, to have to meet stupid people every day, to have to listen to their trivial conversation!" (*Vanya*, 203). Arkadina of *The Seagull* ridicules this provincial tedium: "Oh, what could be more boring than this cloying country boredom! So hot, so still, nobody does anything, everybody talking like a philosopher" (*Seagull*, 141). Therefore, it is argued that Chekhov's plays dramatize "how the daily routine gradually shrinks the spirit and drains the will" (Brockett, 323). And Chekhov's plays usually end where they begin; "the leaden dullness of this sterile country existence repeats itself as it began" (Pedrotti, 245). When a Chekhov play opens, his characters are seen as a part of a monotonous life, and throughout the play they try to struggle with this monotony, which makes them unhappy and miserable individuals. Consequently, the play ends with the same unhappy individuals of the beginning, who are still inert and unproductive, still unfulfilled and unhappy. In Chekhov's plays "life is not a lineal movement toward a finite goal, but a process of endless striving, suffering, fall and recovery" (Jackson, 16). His characters are too passive to struggle with their frustrations, with the riddle of life; so they are deprived of meaningful goals and happiness. When they become disillusioned, in a futile attempt, they try to recover themselves to run after happiness again.

The Three Sisters opens with the sisters' hopes for the future. Nevertheless, in the last act, Olga concludes, "nothing happens," when the sisters end where they begin without having realized their aims (*Sisters*, 325). Masha returns to her husband after a secret love affair with Vershinin, and Irena to her loneliness after the death of her fiancée. Emphasizing the similarity between the play's beginning and ending, Eugene K. Bristow asserts in his essay that "the life cycle starts over against the end. And the ending resembles the beginning" (91). In *The Cherry Orchard*, Liubov and Gayev come together to save their estate but at the end of the play they return to where they come from without having achieved anything. Annia keeps saying that it is a beginning of a new life, but it is just "the cyclic repetition of the old," opposes Senelick (125). The characters themselves are responsible for their entrapment into a vicious circle since they choose to be passive individuals: "The sense of doom and of guilt that weighs upon Liubov and Gayev is not alone in the face of circumstances, […] it is in them, in their passive nature, in their philosophy" (Jackson, 10).

The Chekhovian cyclic lifestyle is observable in several of Ayckbourn's plays in which the characters end where they begin, unable to survive life's changes. *Woman in Mind* opens with darkness, with Susan moaning as she regains consciousness. The audience is first introduced with her fantasy family and witnesses one of the happiest marriages in Ayckbourn's drama. However, when her real family takes place, diametrically opposed to the hallucinatory one, Susan's predicament comes to the surface. We have argued that she feels desperate due to an uncomprehending husband, lack of definite roles and of a proper job to define her identity, and alienation. She is disillusioned with her marriage and with the wretched life she leads in general; however, she has neither the power nor the capacity of changing her lot. Like Chekhov's characters, she is trapped in a vicious circle where she strives, suffers alone, falls and tries to recover vainly. At the end of the play, she is again in darkness, more isolated and more suffering, this time losing her consciousness: "Susan gives a last despairing wail. As she does so, the lights fade to Black-out" (*Mind*, 61).

In *Henceforward*, Jerome leads a miserable and lonely life, struggling in vain to produce the feeling of love with his keyboards; but he is unable to identify the real human feeling of love. In the end, his wife offers reconciliation and asks him to come back and live with his family; it is an offer of love and care, yet he refuses to recognize this humane feeling, and the play ends when Jerome turns again to his computers to express the feeling of love mechanically. Therefore, the play ends as it begins; Jerome chooses to live with machines rather than human beings: "He sits all alone. And realizes how alone he is" (*Henceforward*, 98). The monotony of life, in *Season's Greetings*, is stressed with the symbolic use of the TV show that the characters watch every year. It is an old film, and they remember watching it many times before:

> Harvey: This is a marvelous film, you know. Marvelous.
> Bernard: I think I've seen before, haven't I?
> Harvey: (slightly irritably) What's that?
> Bernard: I said, I have a feeling that this has been on TV before. Hasn't it?
> Harvey: Probably. I think it was on last Christmas. Matter of fact, I think it's on every Christmas. It's very old.
> (*Greetings*, 1-2)

Like the film on TV, life, to them, repeats itself with the same dull routine. Everything they do, they do it every Christmas and did it all the past Christmases. Belinda reminds Bernard that the big presents will be given to the children on Boxing Day as usual, as they did it last year (*Greetings*, 2), and Bernard does not want to be drown into a discussion with Harvey this year as he did in the previous years (*Greetings*, 3). Then, every year on Boxing Day, Bernard does a puppet show, in which nobody is interested, and "it's become rather traditional" (*Greetings*, 7). Christmas, rather than a bonding experience and an occasion to look forward to for the whole family, is a time of boring, burdensome and harassing get-together, repeated every after year.

Choosing to Be

The characters in both dramatists' plays choose to be passive; therefore, they are in themselves open to the element of defeat. Moreover, they contribute to their entrapment into an indeterminate condition through their own action, or rather inaction, for "the objective passiveness of [them] in fact leaves everything open to counterproductive chance" (Jackson, 10). Chekhov's drama renders characters wholly in the power of chance; but it is well-known by the reader that fate, chance or luck, of course, is not going to bring the sisters to Moscow, or save the cherry orchard. Ayckbourn's drama, too, reflects fate-bound individuals who "are frequently at the mercy of random collisions and chance events" (Billington, 51). Thus, both playwrights' characters are not able to change their destinies.

What irritates Chekhov is the passive nature of his characters, and the fact that they easily find themselves at the mercy of other forces and in utter boredom. However, the playwright "prefers the active responsibilities contingent on accepting one's lot, even if this means a fate like Nina's" (Senelick, 87). An existentialist viewpoint is present in Chekhov's plays in that in his drama it is clear "man fashions his own existence and only exists by so doing, and, in that process, and by the choice of what he does or does not do, gives essence to that existence" (Cuddon, 295). A momentary situation or a chance event may overturn lives of Chekhov's characters; nonetheless, they themselves are the determining force. Their lives would be determined by something more than the arbitrariness of chance, and that is the characters themselves, the "process of choosing himself to be" (Esslin, 26). Sartre is the most widely influential figure of modern existentialism, and in Sartre's vision man is born into a kind of mud, and unaware of his situation. He has the liberty to remain in this condition and lead a passive, lazy existence, accepting it without questioning —as Chekhov's and Ayckbourn's characters do. However, he may free himself from this passive and indeterminate condition; he has the energy to "drag himself out of the mud," presupposes Sartre (qtd. in Cuddon, 295). So man has the power of choice either to lead a passive or active existence, and by his decisions and choices, he "makes himself what he is, and has to be what he is" (Cuddon, 295).

The only way to escape from the entrapment of the vicious circle for Chekhov's characters is, first of all, to make a decision and to act according to his or her choice, to be the dominating power in their own lives. Nina in Chekhov's *The Seagull* is the only character who manages to free herself from the entrapment. She "can be singled out as the one survivor who preserves her ideals in spite of all" (Senelick, 75). Unlike any other Chekhovian character, she is not ruled by her inertia, so she can realize her aim. Unlike Konstantin, she never becomes the victim of passiveness or other obstacles, and she does not lose her power to overcome these obstacles. She thoroughly remains constant to her purpose in a determined way in spite of difficulties: "Nina compromises her fantasies by persevering, though aware that stardom is out of her reach" (Senelick, 82). In the end, she succeeds in becoming an actress despite her father. Although she does not become a famous actress, she becomes a self-assertive individual. Robert Louis Jackson sees Nina's strength of making decisions as her only weapon with which she destroys the hostile forces that try to block her goal and comes out of the senseless circumstances and limitations (8). Nina declares:

> I've decided irrevocably, the die is cast —I'm going on the stage. I shall be gone from here tomorrow, I'm leaving my father, leaving everything, I'm beginning a new life.
>
> (*Seagull*, 164)

Chekhov's Nina prefigures Pam in Ayckbourn's *Just Between Ourselves*. Like Nina, Pam is able to free herself from her marital yoke and wretched life by her ability to make decisions. She plans to take a degree course in order to teach, no more believing that her marital life is an obstacle on her way. She realizes she has to do something with her life, and she goes for it: She will work on her qualifications, launch a career, and separate from her husband, which other Ayckbourn characters dare not do. For example, Vera, in contrast, is defeated by her inertia, "by the fortyish feeling that, in her unqualified state, it is too late to get another job" (Billington, 115).

In spite of the abundance of inactive and lackadaisical characters, both Chekhov and Ayckbourn introduce a few active characters who can fight against the odds and shape their lives the way they yearn for; they take control of their own lives. These characters are used as foils to the assembly of inactive men and women that inhabit the plays. In the final analysis, both dramatists see man as determining his own course rather than being at the mercy of environment and circumstances. Sartre's dictum, "man makes himself," can be applicable to both Chekhov's and Ayckbourn's characters. What the characters "make themselves" becomes really pitiful. The few courageous ones like Nina and Pam serve to expose, even more, the impotent majority.

CONCLUSION

Alan Ayckbourn's characters have been analyzed in terms of Chekhovian character traits in this book to show the impact of Chekhovian character portrayal on Ayckbourn's drama. Three major character traits are distinguished in Chekhov's drama which are observed to be widely shared by Ayckbourn. In Chekhov's character portrayal, the trait of inertia among them is the most dominant one, for it comes to be the initializing feature for other traits; the passive streak in the nature of Chekhov's characters is the main element depriving them of fulfillment. Chekhov's characters are seen as inactive people who refuse change of any sort in their static lives. In the plays analyzed, Ayckbourn's characters also appear with a similar lethargic nature when compared with those of Chekhov's, and they are physically as well as mentally inept individuals. It is seen that Chekhov's and Ayckbourn's characters are lazy in a leisurely-fashion and emotionally stagnant to understand each other or to be sensitive to the others' needs and plights. Both playwrights' characters prove to be unproductive individuals and parasitic by nature. The characters' inertia makes them dependent figures who feed off the others' lives and enthusiasm like a sponge. When characters realize that they have been exploited by their fellowmen, they feel that their lives are wasted and unlived, which they find unbearable. The unproductivity of the characters makes them superfluous men and women, living on for no purpose and unneeded by others.

The implausible discontentment with life is analyzed as another trait that Ayckbourn shares with Chekhov. In Chekhov's plays, his characters suffer from dissatisfaction with life so much that it becomes their characteristic feature; and the same feature is present in Ayckbourn's characters, too, in that his characters are equally disillusioned and unhappy individuals without any apparent reason they can reckon. Both playwrights' characters are defined as frustrated individuals; and their inertia is discussed as the only real frustrating factor. The outside forces are the excuses that the characters hide their impotency behind. It is discussed in this work that the disillusioned characters of both dramatists find the realities bitter and hostile, and that they systematically reinterpret them according to their wishes. Thus, they create a relatively smoother world that they can easily cope with. This is seen as an escape mechanism and as the reason for them to create their dream worlds.

Alienation is the modern man's plight. It is stated in this study that Ayckbourn's lonely characters are prefigured in Chekhov's plays. Chekhov is able to observe the lack of communication between human beings and to portray his characters as lonely individuals by nature. Following the Chekhovian trait, it is asserted in the plays analyzed that Ayckbourn's characters are alienated from each other as well as from their selves due to lack of communication among his characters. Furthermore, both dramatists' characters are defined as tongue-tied individuals since they are equally unable and reluctant to express their emotions and thoughts. They do not want to share any of their feelings with their fellowmen, and they consciously retreat themselves into their own isolated worlds.

Such characters, inactive both physically and mentally, avoid change. In Chekhov's plays there is the looming change of the Revolution as an outside force whereas in Ayckbourn's plays there is no imminent social change. However, both playwrights are more concerned with human being's innate fear of and reaction to change. They are unproductive, unfulfilled as they are unable to reach any of their wishes, let alone persevering their aims. They are disillusioned, isolated as they are incapable of relating to their fellowmen, and alienated from their own identity. They are, in fact, "the modern man" depicted on the stage. These individuals are thought to be the products of Absurd Drama, emerging after the horrors of World War II. Nevertheless, long before the two World Wars, they were also observed and portrayed by Chekhov at a time just before the dawn of the Russian Revolution. Thus, such a character depiction does not belong only to Absurd Drama and/or post-modern fiction. Chekhov, too, has a remarkable insight into the human nature and is sensitive to the spiritual and mental collapse of modern man. He is able to discern the plight of man and to reflect what is hidden deep down in him. His aim is to show mankind "how badly [we] live, and how tiresome [we] are," and to indicate that man does not do anything to destroy this vicious circle. The intention of Ayckbourn drama is along Chekhovian lines —to reveal ourselves to ourselves. His plays, too, are the masterful explorations of man's dreary present life. Like Chekhov, he writes plays concerned with "spiritual and mental collapse" of man, as he puts forward in his preface to *Just Between Ourselves*.

The usual characters that crowd both dramatists' plays suffer under the burden of being —to exist becomes an unbearable burden for them. With such a painful burden, they would even be prone to suicide in Chekhov's drama and to mental breakdown in that of Ayckbourn. Although Chekhov insists that his plays are "comedies," he offers no solution to his characters' plight as expected in a comedy. Ayckbourn, following his "master's" footsteps, offers no happy ending. In fact, Ayckbourn's comedy can very likely end up with a character at the brink of mental breakdown, catatonia or schizophrenia. In both playwrights' view of man, the language being adequate for communication is man's tragedy. The character depiction of their dramas fuses comedy and tragedy, creating modern "human comedies".

BIBLIOGRAPHY

Ayckbourn, Alan. *Absent Friends*. London: Penguin Books, 1979.

_____ *Henceforward*. London: Faber and Faber Ltd., 1989.

_____ "*Joking Apart.*" *Joking Apart and Other Plays*. London: Penguin Books, 1988.

_____ "*Just Between Ourselves.*' *Joking Apart and Other Plays*. London: Penguin Books, 1988.

_____ *Season's Greetings*. London: Samuel French Ltd., 1982.

_____ *A Small Family Business*. London: Faber and Faber Ltd., 1989.

_____ *Woman in Mind*. London: Samuel French, 1987.

Baker, Stuart E. "Ayckbourn and the Tradition of Farce." Dukore 25-40.

Barricelli, Jean-Pierre, ed. *Chekhov's Great Plays*: *A Critical Anthology*. New York: New York University Press, 1981.

Bently, Eric. "Craftsmanship in *Uncle Vanya*." Eekman 169-185.

Billington, Michael. *Alan Ayckbourn*. London: Macmillan, 1990.

Bordinat, Philip. "Dramatic Structure in Chekhov's *Uncle Vanya*." Barricelli 47-60.

Bristow, Eugene K. "Circles, Triads, and Parity in The Three Sisters." Barricelli 76-95.

Brockett, Oscar G. *The Theatre: An Introduction*. New York: Holt, Rineheart and Winston, Inc., 1974.

Chakraborty, Bhaktibenode. *Anton Chekhov: The Crusader for a Better World*. New Delhi: K P Bagchi & Company, 1990.

Chekhov, Anton. "*The Cherry Orchard.*" *Plays*: *Anton Chekhov*. London: Penguin Books, 1959.

_____ "*The Seagull.*" *Plays*: *Anton Chekhov*. London: Penguin Books, 1959.

_____ "*The Three Sisters.*" *Plays*: *Anton Chekhov*. London: Penguin Books, 1959.

_____ "*Uncle Vanya.*" *Plays*: *Anton Chekhov*. London: Penguin Books, 1959.

Coleman, James C. *Abnormal Psychology and Modern Life*. London: Stuart, 1980.

Cuddon, J. A., ed. *The Penguin Dictionary of Literary Terms and Literary Theory*. London: Penguin Books, 1999.

Dukore, Bernard F, ed. *Alan Ayckbourn: A Casebook*. London: Garland Publishing, Inc., 1991.

Eagleton, Terry. *Literary Theory*. Oxford: Blackwell Publishers, 1996.

Eekman, Thomas A., ed. *Critical Essays on Anton Chekhov*. Boston: G. K. Hall & Co., 1989.

Esslin, Martin. *The Theatre of the Absurd*. New York: Anchor Books, 1961.

Fay, Stephen. "Alan Ayckbourn Interview: At Home with the Human Heart." *Independent on Sunday* 4 Nov. 1999: 4.

Holt, Michael. *Alan Ayckbourn*. Plymouth: Northcote House, 1999.

Hornby, Richard. "Ayckbourn's Men." Dukore 103-113.

Jackson, Robert Louis. "Chekhov's *Seagull*: The Empty Well, the Dry Lake, and the Cold Cave." Barricelli 3-17.

Josephson, Eric, ed. *Man Alone: Alienation in Modern Society*. New York: Dell Pub Co., 1962.

Kalson, Albert E. *Laughter in the Dark*. London: Associated University Press, 1993.

Kirca, Mustafa. "Language in Ayckbourn's Plays". *Journal of Drama Studies*. Vol.2, No.2. Delhi: Primus Books, 2008. 129-138.

Lodge, David. *20th Century Literary Criticism: A Reader*. London: Longman, 1972.

Londré, Felicia Hardison. "Ayckbourn's Women." Dukore 87-101.

Magarshack, David. *Chekhov the Dramatist*. London: Eyre Methuen Ltd., 1980.

Martin, Barclay. *Anxiety and Neurotic Disorders*. London: John Wiley & Sons, 1971.

Meister, Charles W. *Chekhov Criticism: 1880 Through 1986*. London: McFarland & Company, Inc., Publishers, 1988.

Nilsson, Nils Ake. "Two Chekhovs: Mayakovskiy on Chekhov's 'Futurism'." Barricelli 251-262.

Page, Malcolm. "The Serious Side of Alan Ayckbourn." Zeifman 134-146.

Paperny, Zinovii S. "Microsubjects in *The Seagull*." Eekman 160-168.

Peace, Richard. "An Introduction to Chekhov's Plays." Eekman 126-138.

Pedrotti, Louis. "Chekhov's Major Plays: A Doctor in the House." Barricelli 233-250.

Senelick, Laurence. *Anton Chekhov*. London: Macmillan, 1985.

Stavrakakis, Yannis. *Lacan & The Political*. London: Routledge, 1999.

Styan, John L. "*The Cherry Orchard*." Eekman 192-200.

Valency, Maurice. "*The Three Sisters*." Eekman 186-191.

Vitins, Ieva. "Uncle Vanya's Predicament." Barricelli 35-46.

Watson, Ian. *Conversations With Ayckbourn*. London: Macdonald Futura Ltd., 1981.

Weston, Drew. *Psychology: Mind, Brain & Culture*. New York: John Wiley & Sons, Inc., 1996.

Wright, Elizabeth E. *Psychoanalytic Criticism*. London: Methuen, 1984.

Yarmolinsky, Avrahm. *The Portable Chekhov*. New York: The Viking.

Youssef, Christine. *Dissatisfied and Distraught Woman in Alan Ayckbourn's Plays*. Diss. Middle East Technical U, 1993.

Zeifman, Hersh, ed. *Contemporary British Drama*. London: Macmillan, 1993

Zoglin, Richard. "Ayckbourn's Conquest." *Time* 28 Aug. 2000: 60.

"The Unbearable Lightness of Ayckbourn." *Economist* 7 March 1998: 87.

INDEX

absurd **8, 63**; Absurd Drama **63, 87**

Anouilh, Jean **5**

Ayckbourn, Alan **1, 2, 5, 6, 7, 8, 9, 11, 12, 16, 23, 24, 25, 27, 29, 30, 31, 33, 35, 36, 37, 39, 40, 41, 42, 43, 44, 45, 46, 47, 49, 50, 51, 52, 53, 54, 55, 56, 57, 58, 59, 60, 61, 63, 64, 65, 66, 67, 68, 69, 71, 72, 73, 74, 75, 76, 77, 79, 80, 82, 83, 84, 85, 86, 87**

A Small Family Business **9, 51, 52, 59, 61, 67, 68, 69, 71, 72**

Absent Friends **6, 7, 8, 9, 13, 14, 29, 34, 35, 47, 51, 56, 57, 66, 67, 68, 72**

Garden **7**

Henceforward **9, 23, 24, 25, 27, 54, 55, 59, 81**

House **7**

Joking Apart **9, 24, 27, 30, 60, 61, 62**

Just Between Ourselves **9, 13, 29, 30, 33, 34, 35, 36, 37, 38, 39, 40, 41, 43, 45, 46, 50, 52, 53, 67, 72, 73, 76, 77, 84, 87**

Relatively Speaking **6**

Season's Greetings **9, 30, 56, 57, 58, 73, 81, 82**

Woman in Mind **9, 13, 25, 26, 36, 37, 38, 39, 40, 41, 43, 46, 47, 53, 54, 60, 69, 77, 80, 81**

Baker, Stuart E. **7, 8**

Barricelli, Jean-Pierre **68**

Bently, Eric **69**

Billington, Michael **9, 24, 35, 36, 37, 38, 53, 55, 59, 61, 72, 76, 82, 84**

Bordinat, Philip **33**

Bristow, Eugene K. **80**

Brockett, Oscar G. **42, 79**

Chakraborty, Bhaktibenode **17**

Chekhov, Anton **1, 2, 5, 6, 7, 8, 9, 11, 12, 13, 14, 15, 16, 17, 19, 20, 22, 23, 24, 25, 27, 28, 29, 30, 31, 32, 33, 35, 42, 44, 45, 46, 47, 49, 50, 51, 55, 56, 58, 59, 60, 61, 63, 64, 65, 68, 69, 70, 71, 73, 74, 75, 77, 79, 80, 82, 83, 84, 85, 86, 87**

   Cherry Orchard, The **8, 9, 12, 13, 14, 15, 17, 19, 20, 21, 22, 23, 24, 27, 28, 29, 45, 68, 70, 71, 76, 77, 80, 82,**

   Seagull, The **9, 28, 29, 31, 32, 33, 43, 50, 56, 58, 60, 79, 83, 84**

   Three Sisters, The **9, 12, 19, 29, 32, 33, 42, 43, 44, 45, 47, 51, 56, 70, 71, 73, 75, 76, 80, 82**

   Uncle Vanya **9, 15, 16, 17, 18, 19, 20, 21, 22, 23, 24, 29, 33, 44, 49, 50, 51, 58, 59, 65, 66, 79**

Coleman, James C. **44, 45, 46,**

Comedy **1, 5, 6, 7, 8, 9, 35, 58, 87**; Chekhovian comedy **5, 8**; human comedies **5, 6, 87**

Cuddon, J. A. **82, 83**

Dukore, Bernard F. **5**

Eagleton, Terry **64, 65, 74, 75**

Eekman, Thomas A. **11, 12, 32**

Esslin, Martin **63, 83**

Farce, farcical **1, 6, 7, 8**

Fay, Stephen **68**

Hare, David **1**

Holt, Michael **54**

Ibsen, Henrik **5**

Ionesco, Eugene **5**

Jackson, Robert Louis **80, 82, 83**

Josephson, Eric **54, 74**

Kalson, Albert E. **5, 77**

Kirca, Mustafa **63**

Kugel, A. R. **28**

Lacan, Jacques **64, 65, 75**

Lodge, David **65**

Londré, Felicia Hardison **35, 36, 39, 46**

Magarshack, David **6, 20, 28, 29, 56, 58, 69, 71**

Martin, Barclay **46**

McCarthy, Desmond **28**

Meister, Charles W. **69**

Nilsson, Nils Ake **70, 76**

Page, Malcolm **6, 7, 8**

Paperny, Zinovii S. **47**

Peace, Richard **72**

Pedrotti, Louis **79**

Pinter, Harold **1, 5, 63**

Pirandello, Luigi **5**

Sartre, Jean-Paul **83, 84**

Saussure, Ferdinand **64**

Senelick, Laurence **14, 16, 18, 22, 28, 42, 43, 44, 45, 66, 80, 82, 83**

Shakespeare, William **2**

Stavrakakis, Yannis **74**

Stoppard, Tom **1**

Styan, John L. **8**

Tragedy **1, 2, 6, 7, 8, 87**
Valency, Maurice **11, 14, 32, 47**
Vitins, Ieva **18**
Watson, Ian **5, 40**
Weston, Drew **64**
Wright, Elizabeth E. **64**
Yarmolinsky, Avrahm **45**
Youssef, Christine **34, 52, 63**
Zoglin, Richard **7**

ibidem-Verlag

Melchiorstr. 15

D-70439 Stuttgart

info@ibidem-verlag.de

www.ibidem-verlag.de
www.ibidem.eu
www.edition-noema.de
www.autorenbetreuung.de